2666

Daughters of St. Paul

<u>HEAVEN</u>

1. Heaven

HEAVEN

Heaven

by the
Daughters of St. Paul

St. Paul Editions

IMPRIMATUR:

✦ Humberto Cardinal Medeiros
Archbishop of Boston

February 15, 1977

Photo Credits:

Alvarez, 127
ENIT, 75
Sahata, 143

Library of Congress Cataloging in Publication Data

Daughters of St. Paul.
    Heaven.

        1. Heaven.   2. Christian life — Catholic authors.
I. Title.
BT846.2.D38   1977   248'.48'2   77-4669

Printed in U.S.A. by the Daughters of St. Paul
50 St. Paul's Ave., Boston, Ma. 02130

The Daughters of St. Paul are an international
religious congregation serving the Church with
the communications media.

To the Most Holy Virgin,
Gracious Star and Gate of Heaven

It trains us to reject godless ways and worldly desires, and live temperately, justly, and devoutly in this age as we await our blessed hope, the appearing of the glory of the great God and of our Savior Christ Jesus.

(Titus 2:12-13)

CONTENTS

Foreword

The author asked me to write a few words of introduction; she requests that this be based on theology....

I comply by dedicating to her a little incident of practical—yet exalted—theology, of perennial philosophy, of purest aesthetics, of original mysticism, of spiritual life, and of eremitic flavor.

While St. Francis de Sales was visiting his diocese, he was told of a good peasant who was ill and wished to receive the saint's blessing before he died. The saint immediately went to see him, and found a venerable old man facing death with the greatest serenity of mind.

"Your Excellency," said the sick man upon seeing him, "praised be God for giving me the chance of receiving your blessing before I close my eyes forever."

Then he asked St. Francis to hear his confession. Everyone else left the room, and after confession, while he was still alone with the bishop, the old man asked point blank, "Your Excellency, am I going to die?"

"My dear friend," answered St. Francis, "a doctor can tell you better than I."

"But I'm asking your opinion, Your Excellency. What do you think? Am I going to die?"

"Everyone must die, and the moment is uncertain. As for you, it's not absolutely certain that your hour has come. Others have been known to recover who were more dangerously ill than you are."

"Your Excellency," the old man resumed, "don't think I'm asking you this because I'm afraid to die. Far from it—I'm afraid that I might not die now."

The saint was surprised by these words. He knew that the desire for death comes only to the most perfect souls, as also to some of the most imperfect, who have fallen into the depths of despair.

"Then, you're not unhappy about dying?" St. Francis asked the sick man.

"So little so that if God had not wanted me to stay at my post until He called me, I would have been long gone."

"But why such a dislike for life? Are you troubled by secret sorrows, physical sufferings, bankruptcy...?"

"Not at all. I'm seventy, and till now I've had fine health. And I've got more things than I need; God hasn't given me any taste of poverty."

"Maybe there's trouble in your family, with your wife or children?"

"Far from it. I'm as happy as can be. My wife and children have never displeased me. If anything were to make me suffer, it would be having to leave them."

"But, then," marveled St. Francis, "my brother in the Lord, why do you want to die?"

"Your Excellency, in sermons I've often heard about the wonders of the future life and the joys of heaven. So, the present life really seems like a prison to me!"

At this point, out of the fullness of his heart, the sick man said such marvelous and touching things about the splendor of heaven and the emptiness of earthly goods, that the holy bishop was moved to tears.

St. Francis reconfirmed him in those noble sentiments, asked him to repeat the acts of resignation and complete submission to the will of God with regard to either living or dying, and administered the Anointing of the Sick.

Soon after that, the virtuous old man expired peacefully, without complaining of any pain. After death an expression of calm sweetness remained on his face, as if his soul, in departing, had imprinted on it the seal of heavenly happiness.

Heaven! He who thinks of it and does not desire it, either has lost his faith, or lost his reason!...

"I believe in life everlasting!" Think of the ascension of Jesus Christ into heaven; think of the assumption of Mary Most Holy into heaven.... There lies the road that is pointed out to the true disciples of the Divine Master!

JAMES ALBERIONE, S.S.P.

PART I

TRUTHS ABOUT HEAVEN

Send forth your light and your fidelity;
*   they shall lead me on*
And bring me to your holy mountain,
to your dwelling-place.

                                        (Ps. 43:3)

CHAPTER I

THERE IS A HEAVEN!

> *I know whom I have
> believed.
> (2 Tm. 1:2)*

When near death, St. Francis of Assisi begged his friars to sing him the "Canticle of the Sun." He joined the choir with his very feeble voice, adding the verse which sings of Sister Death.

Then, as his last moment drew near, with unusual vigor the saint began Psalm 141: "I cry to the Lord with a loud voice," and kept on singing until Sister Death extinguished his voice at the last words: "Bring my soul out of prison.... The just wait for me...."

For St. Francis, before whom the gates of heaven were wide open, all this, which may seem senseless to the atheist, mysterious to the sinner, and strange to the "knight of common sense," was a burning desire of the soul — the desire to chant a hymn of triumph.

Heaven truly exists! If I wished to prove this truth to scholars and theologians, I would compile a Latin treatise with a string of numberless proofs according to the classic order of the doctrine of the Church, Scripture, Tradition, and reason.

But I am writing for the humble, for those who have kept intact the faith they received in Baptism and who, through this simple and pure faith, possess clear and precise notions of eternal truths, and speak with mathematical sureness and infallible certainty

17

of heaven, purgatory and hell as places created by God to receive the soul of man after his earthly pilgrimage.

In fact, they know from the Catholic catechism that *after the particular judgment, if the soul is in the state of grace and free from all sin and from all punishment due to sin, it will go to heaven at once; if it has some venial sins or has not fully satisfied for the temporal punishment due to sins, it will go to purgatory; if it is in a state of mortal sin as an unconverted rebel against God, it will go to hell.*

And this is also the exact doctrine regarding the soul of man after death that the Church has defined through Pope Benedict XII and the Council of Florence.

Therefore, reconfirming these staunch believers in the faith, I shall say to them, "Heaven truly exists!"

We speak and declare with an authority which is based on the Sacred Scriptures, whose pages radiate cheerful heavenly light, and on the infallible teaching of the Church, to whom we humbly yield assent. Further confirmation rests on the universal consensus of all who have never ceased to believe this truth, and on human reason, which demands eternal reward or punishment.

Great souls steeped in undeniable spiritual intuition and deep mystical contemplation, as well as the greatest thinkers and artists, attest to this truth. And as for concrete proof, there are confirmed instances of deceased individuals who have appeared to the living and have borne witness to the reality of heaven.

Heaven truly exists!

In this first chapter we shall confine ourselves simply to proving the existence of heaven as a place of supreme blessedness, in which Jesus Christ in His human nature, the Blessed Virgin, the angels and the saints, dwelling together, enjoy the vision, the delight and the possession of God.

St. Paul speaks of heaven as the eternal dwelling of the soul: "Indeed, we know that when the earthly tent in which we dwell is destroyed we have a dwelling provided for us by God, a dwelling in the heavens, not made by hands but to last forever" (2 Cor. 5:1). And in the liturgy of the dead, sublime in the concept of death for us Christians, the Church prays:

"Lord, for your faithful people, life is changed, not ended.

When the body of our earthly dwelling lies in death we gain an everlasting dwelling place in heaven" (Preface for the Dead).

In the Book of Revelation, St. John describes heaven as the new Jerusalem, the holy city in which God dwells among men and sheds His light upon them as they look upon His face. "Nothing deserving a curse shall be found there. The throne of God and of the Lamb shall be there, and his servants shall serve him faithfully. They shall see him face to face and bear his name on their foreheads. The night shall be no more. They will need no light from lamps or the sun, for the Lord God shall give them light, and they shall reign forever" (Rv. 22:3-5).

As for the place where heaven is, nothing certain is known about it.

Generally, theologians teach that it is a place in the universe, but relatively superior to ours.

St. Albert the Great describes this place thus: "Heaven is...most simple in nature, very subtle in essence, most solid in incorruptibility, maximum in quantity and most pure in matter." But wherever it may be located, it suffices us to know the way that leads to it, and the sure way that leads us to heaven is Christ — the Way, the Truth and the Life. In following Him, we shall surely reach heaven.

Definite Indications

We read in the Sacred Scriptures that when Moses came down from Mount Sinai with the tables of the law, two rays of light shone from his face, "because of his familiar conversation with God." Seeing his radiant face, the people did not dare go near him. After having given the law to the children of Israel, he covered his face with a veil. "Whenever Moses entered the presence of the Lord to converse with him, he removed the veil until he came out again. On coming out, he would tell the Israelites all that had been commanded. Then the Israelites would see that the skin of Moses' face was radiant; so he would again put the veil over his face until he went in to converse with the Lord" (Ex. 34:34-35).

The marvelous event of the transfiguration, as related by Matthew in chapter 17, was a reflection of the splendor of heaven: "Six days later, Jesus took with him Peter and James and his brother John and led them up a high mountain where they could be alone. There in their presence he was transfigured: his face shone like the sun and his clothes became as white as the light. Suddenly Moses and Elijah appeared to them; they were talking with him. Then Peter spoke to Jesus. 'Lord,' he said, 'it is wonderful for us to be here; if you wish, I will make three tents here, one for you, one for Moses and one for Elijah'" (Mt. 17:1-4) (JB).

In the New Testament, Jesus often spoke, both with parables and directly, of the kingdom of heaven, to which the just will go and where they will see God.

Thus, in the sermon on the mount, He called the poor of spirit and those who suffer persecution for justice' sake blessed: "the reign of God is theirs." "Blest are the single-hearted for they shall see God." And to those who are persecuted for the faith He says: "Be glad and rejoice, for your reward is great in heaven" (Mt. 5:3, 8, 12).

Elsewhere, condemning the Pharisees' pride in coveting titles, Jesus admonished: "Do not call anyone on earth your father. Only one is your father, the One in heaven" (Mt. 23:9).

And to the good thief who begged Him to remember him when He entered His kingdom, Jesus answered: "I assure you: this day you will be with me in paradise" (Lk. 23:43).

At the last judgment, after the unchangeable sentence, He will say: "Come. You have my Father's blessing! Inherit the kingdom prepared for you from the creation of the world" (Mt. 25:34).

The promise He made to the apostles before ascending to heaven is explicit: "Do not let your hearts be troubled. Have faith in God and faith in me. In my Father's house there are many dwelling places; otherwise, how could I have told you that I was going to prepare a place for you? I am indeed going to prepare a place for you, and then I shall come back to take you with me, that where I am you also may be" (Jn. 14:1-3).

There is really no point, however, in going on to mention other separate proofs. At least 400 times, holy Scripture speaks of heaven as our ultimate end. Almost all the parables hint at it.

Jesus came to earth to reopen the gates of this blessed kingdom for us. Every divine teaching is directed to its conquest, and the Son of God gave us the proof of blood, so to speak, thus assuring us of its possession at the price of His passion and His death on the cross.

Belief in a future life, where virtue shall be rewarded, has always been alive among all peoples, even pagans.

This belief also conforms with reason. In fact, is it not justice for one who does evil to be punished and one who does good to be rewarded? Isn't that the way things are supposed to be in this world? Moreover, in reciting the Apostles' Creed daily, we profess that we "believe in God, the Father almighty, Creator of heaven and earth." And we conclude with a declaration of faith in "life everlasting."

Heaven truly exists!

Conclusive Facts

St. John Bosco's biography records that in the year 1860, in a very consoling vision, he saw his mother Margaret, who had been dead for some time. She was lively and smiling.

"Mother—you, here?" Don Bosco said to her. "But, you're not dead, then?"

"Yes, I am dead," answered his mother, "but I live!"

"Are you happy?"

"Very!"

"In heaven?"

"In heaven!...although I have passed through the flames of purgatory."

Don Bosco asked other questions: "Are any of our boys in heaven?"

"Yes, many." And she named several of them.

"What do you enjoy there?"

"You're asking the impossible," she answered. "No one can ever describe or express what we enjoy in heaven."

Then suddenly a light of inexplicable beauty enveloped her, and exclaiming, "John, I'll be waiting for you to be with me forever in paradise!" she disappeared amid the heavenly harmony of thousands and thousands of angelic voices.

One day, when the disconsolate parents of the Roman patrician Agnes were weeping at their daughter's tomb, Agnes herself appeared before them. She was all radiant, and a band of virgins singing hosannas accompanied her. "Dear parents," she said, "Don't weep as if I were dead. Together with these virgins, I enjoy a new life in heaven near Him whom I loved with all my heart when I was on earth."

Heaven truly exists!

This comforting reality is also upheld by two more episodes, taken from the life of the angelic doctor, St. Thomas Aquinas.

In the life of this saint, we read that one day the soul of one of his sisters, who had died in the convent of St. Mary of Capua, of which she was the abbess, appeared to him in all the splendor of triumphant glory. Familiar as he had become with supernatural things, the saint did not hesitate to ask the apparition news of his two brothers, Arnold and Landolph, also dead for some time.

"As for Landolph," his sister replied, "he is still in purgatory, where he's suffering greatly and is much in need of suffrages. Arnold is in heaven," she continued, "and enjoys a high degree of glory there because of his defense of the Church and of the Pope against the unholy aggressions of Emperor Frederick. As for you, my dear brother," she added, "a magnificent place is reserved for you as a reward for all that you have done for the Church. Hurry to give the last touch to the various works you have begun, for very soon you will be united with us."

History tells us that he died shortly afterwards.

While praying in the Church of St. Dominic in Naples on another occasion, the same saint saw one of his confreres approaching him. It was Romanus, his successor in the chair of theology at Paris.

Not knowing that Romanus had died, Thomas at first thought he had just come from Paris. So he rose, went to meet him, greeted him, and asked news of his health and the reason for his journey.

"I am no longer of this world," the friar smilingly informed him, "and through the mercy of God, I already enjoy the possession of the Supreme Good; by His order I have come to encourage you in your works."

"Am I in the state of grace?" asked Thomas at once.

"Yes, my brother, and your works are very pleasing to God."

"And you, did you pass through purgatory?"

"Yes, for fifteen days, because of various infidelities not sufficiently atoned for before."

Always preoccupied with theological questions, Thomas wanted to avail himself of this opportunity in order to clear up the mystery of the Beatific Vision, but the answer he received was a verse from Psalm 48: "As we had heard, so have we seen in the city of the Lord of hosts, in the city of our God" (v. 9).

With these words, the apparition vanished, leaving the angelic doctor on fire with a great desire for heaven.

The first man to be given the privilege of seeing heaven while he was still here below was the proto-martyr, St. Stephen. Just before the excruciating torment of his martyrdom, heaven opened to him and his gaze fixed itself upon the Son of God, standing at the right hand of the Father.

And the first person who was able to penetrate into heaven while still living was St. Paul. He afterwards wrote of having heard there "words which cannot be uttered, words which no man may speak" (2 Cor. 12:4).

But we poor mortals are still pilgrims, to whom it is not given to enjoy the visions which Stephen and Paul had: "Now we see indistinctly, as in a mirror" (1 Cor. 13:12). When it will please the Lord to take us from the prison of this life, then we shall see "face to face."

However, those same truths are offered to us for our meditation by our Christian faith.

How many individuals who lead lives of obscurity, and often of suffering, have come to know through grace what these two saints experienced through visions.

Intuitions of Heaven

St. Agatha, a virgin of Catania, ardently sought in marriage by many illustrious personages because of her beauty and wealth, heroically rejected their dazzling offers and preferred martyrdom, as she looked forward to her eternal reward.

St. Ignatius of Loyola used to spend his nights on the terrace of the house of the professed in Rome, from which he would contemplate the beautiful, starry sky and say, as his soul was flooded with heavenly light and sweetness: "Oh, how worthless the earth seems when I contemplate the sky!"

"My son, look up at heaven!" said the heroic mother of the Maccabees to her last-born child, as she exhorted him to endure martyrdom.

More recent occurrences are not lacking.

Even in our day, although it seems that man has forgotten his eternal destiny, there are souls, chiefly young souls, who have an intuition of heaven. Their enthusiasm for all that is holy, noble and beautiful tells us that they foresee eternal happiness.

Argene Fati, a Franciscan tertiary and promoter of the Young Girls of Catholic Action, who died in Rome on August 13, 1926, said on her deathbed, "I must strive not to think of heaven, for at the mere thought of it, my heart beats violently from excess of happiness. I too, like our Father St. Francis, sing: 'Be praised, my Lord, for sister bodily death.'"

And, knowing that her friends were praying for her recovery, she would say: "They are asking for a miracle.... But I have a great desire to go to heaven.... I am yearning for the moment when I can go to heaven!..."

Argene was echoed by Ida Mattei, who died in Milan a few months later. She was an elect soul, whose life, inspired by the same Franciscan spirit and consecrated to the same ideal of Catholic Action, was spent seraphically in the love of God.

"Ah, heaven!" Ida exclaimed a few days before her death, "What a burning desire I have for it!" And, after having received the Anointing of the Sick, she added,

"Before, I was merely satisfied to die, but now I am happy…. Yes, let me tell you, I have an intense desire to go…."

On the day before his death, Julius Salvadori, the troubadour of God's beauty, said to his brother, "Tomorrow you will dress me in my best clothes, for it will be the beginning of my days of feasting."

A young student became seriously ill just when he was about to reach his noble ideal. He wanted to live and work for the Church, but when he understood that the Lord wanted him in heaven, he yearned for nothing else.

Shortly before his death, he called his relatives and friends about him, and with a heavenly smile on his face said to them, "Farewell! Good-bye to all of you! Remember me always…. I'm going to heaven!" And, because everyone around him was weeping, he added, "There's no need for you to cry! I'm going to heaven! There I will pray very much for you…. I'm so happy that I'm going to heaven…won't you be glad to go there one day? There we'll always be together…. I'll be waiting for all of you in heaven!"

To those who went to visit him, he would repeat, "Farewell till we meet again in heaven!" And lifting his eyes on high, he would smile as though he were already enjoying its infinite happiness. A few minutes before he died, his sister asked him, "Would you be pleased if, through the Blessed Mother, you were cured?" He shook his head slightly, then looked at the sky and repeated, "No, no, I prefer to die! I want to go to heaven! I want to go to heaven!" A few moments later he passed on.

Not less edifying was the death of a young aspirant of the Daughters of St. Paul. She, too, on her deathbed, seemed to be awaiting the fulfillment of a promise to take part in a celebration. With a radiant face, she would tell everyone who came into her room, "I'm going to heaven! I'm going to heaven!"

Wasted by the ravages of a long illness, a young sister-apostle of the press found such delight at the thought of the nearness of her entry into heaven that when someone somberly spoke to her of resignation to death, she answered energetically, "Be resigned to die? Rather say, 'Be resigned to live!'"

St. Thérèse of the Child Jesus said that, when she was fourteen years old, she had the good fortune of reading the conferences of Abbot Arminjon concerning the end of the present world and the mysteries of the future life. "The reading of that book," declared the saint, "plunged my soul into a joy not of this world; I had already had a foretaste of what God has prepared for those who love Him, and upon viewing those eternal rewards so generously out of proportion to the small sacrifices one makes in this life, I yearned to love—to love Jesus passionately and to give Him a thousand proofs of tenderness for as long a time as possible."*

Souls wholly taken up with the love of God develop an intuitive knowledge of the beauties of heaven and yearn for them. "Blest are the single-hearted, for they shall see God," Jesus said (Mt. 5:8). And St. Thérèse says, "God is heaven."

Wondering at the calmness and fortitude with which the first Christians suffered torture and martyrdom, the pagans believed that they were using anesthetics.

Anesthetics? Yes, they truly were: the thought of a heaven which awaited them.

---

*Story of a Soul

It Is So...

The final end of man is true blessedness, in the attainment of which there is supreme perfection and happiness. In this regard, our reason confirms the judgment of philosophy.

The ultimate end of man is not mere fantasy or only an intangible ideal. It is real, absolute and positive in character. In like manner also, the supreme happiness of man must be real and positive.

What is this deep craving for happiness which everyone experiences within his soul?

In the natural order, we find that there is a reason, a purpose, an objective for everything, even for man's least desire or mental attitude. For instance, the eye was created by God for the purpose of seeing; the ears, for hearing; the legs for moving about; the hands for working and perfecting an infinite number of operations at man's disposal. How, then, can it reasonably be said — without injustice to the infinite wisdom and providence of God — that only that craving for eternal bliss whose roots are deeply imbedded in the human soul must remain forever unsatisfied because it is impossible of attainment? In other words, how can it reasonably be said that heaven does not exist?

The following — strangely enough — is a declaration by that master of unbelief, Victor Hugo. In the French Parliament in the year 1850, during a speech about the need for religious instruction, he gave a memorably splendid defense of the existence of a future life. We quote a few sentences:

"As for me, since fortune willed that I speak at this moment, and that such meaningful words should come from so unauthoritative a person, permit me to say it right here and declare it: I emphatically proclaim it from this tribune: I believe, I profoundly believe in a better world. It is for me much more real than this miserly fantasy that we devour and call life; it is always before my eyes; I believe with all the powers of my conviction, and, after so many struggles, so many studies, and so many proofs, it is the supreme consolation of my soul!''

Future happiness alone will not exert any beneficial influence on our moral life if we do not keep it in mind constantly. It is necessary to think often of heaven. As when on a pilgrimage we keep thinking of the place we are headed for, so in this life's pilgrimage, we must keep thinking of our destination. In this life's pilgrimage, we must turn our mind upward, to the ultimate goal of life, to our true country.

Heaven truly exists!

It is a basic and universal truth.

It is one of the four last things which the Holy Spirit exhorts us to think of in order to keep ourselves from sinning. *"In whatever you do, remember your last days, and you will never sin"* (Sir. 7:36).

The truth of a future life is an inseparable part of faith, a component of human psychology to be reckoned with. It is a truth that must be kept present in every circumstance of life in order to make our joys holy and ward off discouragement in times of trouble. It is a truth that sheds streams of light on human knowledge and solves many a difficult human problem. It is the key that unlocks the mystery of a life sacrificed in secret. It is a truth that fills the drab life of mortal man with hope and happiness and turns his sadness of exile into joyful expectation.

CHAPTER II

WHAT IS HEAVEN?

*Glorious things are said of you, O city
of God!*

(Ps. 87:3)

A Blessed Kingdom

By "heaven," the Church means that state in which
the souls of the just, perfectly purified, enjoy perfect
happiness after death.

The purpose of this book does not call for theological definitions. However, childish ideas and arti-
ficial, too-human descriptions are always to be avoided.
At times, instead of strengthening faith, these lead
to its weakening. Therefore, remaining within the
light of Catholic sacred theology and thus drawing
clarity and certitude from it, I shall present the evi-
dence for heaven in a way that will appeal to the
majority of the faithful, to whom in particular these
pages are dedicated.

One day St. Augustine was seized with an intense desire to see heaven. To him, who was torturing
himself in trying to penetrate the mystery of the Most
Blessed Trinity, this desire did not seem too unreason-
able to pursue.

Troubled by that strong desire, the doctor of the
Church eagerly implored, "O faith, lovable faith,
come to my aid! Tell me what those immense regions
are where God's children stroll. What are the delights
of those blessed shores? Are any flowers there? Is the

air fragrant with rare perfume? Can it be that the nectar and ambrosia that paganism made the food of the false gods are not myths for those who live in heaven?

"We here below are refreshed by the warm breath of welcome breezes. In heaven are there any pleasing, soft winds to delight those happy citizens? Here below, lovely hillsides, green valleys, pleasant fields, sea and skies fill us with delight. What objects do the eyes cherish there? Are they at least partly similar to these we know on earth, or are they entirely new to us?"

To have his doubts cleared, the holy bishop of Hippo calls upon faith: "O holy faith, clear my doubts!"

What does faith answer?

Basing itself on holy Scripture, it tells us:

Heaven is the eternal possession of God, our true happiness, and in Him the possession of every other good, without any evil.

How can this definition be explained?

We might be asked the same question that Diogenes, the cynic, asked of someone who was talking about the marvels of the Elysian Fields: "When did you come back from there?"

The observation has its merits. But when such a truth is met on every page of the sacred Scriptures, when there is no doctor of the Church nor master of the spirit who does not speak of this shining eternal truth, when all the pages of the Gospel abound with mention of heaven, and Jesus Himself has many a time spoken of the kingdom of God, of His Father's home, of the mansions that are waiting there for us; when, according to the words of an excellent religious, "all the teachings of the Gospel, the Fathers and the scholastics are full of heaven," we would indeed be ignorant or indifferent if we did not explain it to everyone.

Let us now proceed to a common objection: "How can we talk about heaven? Who has come back to tell us precisely what it consists of?" We can answer thus: Who has ever gone to the stars that race through the infinity of space? And yet we know their weights and dimensions, their positions and movements; scientists have discovered all that....

Science has inquired into these so-called mysteries, has given them names, has asked of each solar body or planet its innermost secrets. Well, then, is it impossible to believe that the kingdom of heaven, in which God's glory dwells, this kingdom for which man craves with uplifted head and immortal soul, should be spoken of as mere supposition or hypothesis with a possibility of error? It is true that astronomy has constructed powerful telescopes and has arrived at unheard-of calculations with scientific sureness to support its own assertions; but to penetrate the bright spaces of the blessed kingdom, have we not a most powerful lens — faith — which brings the immeasurably far near to the human spirit, a lens reinforced by the infallible proofs of Scripture and Tradition?

The answer that the catechism gives us is marvelously complete. It is a synthesis of tremendous truths expressed in simple words.

It begins with a declaration: "Heaven is the eternal enjoyment of God, our happiness, and in Him of every other good," and ends with a denial: "without any evil." Hence, it proclaims the possession of the greatest Good with the exclusion of any possible evil.

Father Scryvers, a holy religious, speaks thus of heaven:

"Heaven is the eternal possession of the Supreme Good, the fullness of the soul with a happiness that is infinite, substantial, overflowing, the accumulation of all that can make man happy.

"Heaven is the indescribable delight of the senses, the reward for every sacrifice, however small, for every virtuous action, even the most fleeting. Heaven is the gratification of every desire of the soul, a capacity for enjoyment perpetually intense and always fulfilled.

"Heaven is the delight of the spirit, the vision of supernatural mysteries, of their causes and reciprocal relations. It is the knowledge of the wonderful ways of Providence in the government of the world and the behavior of every soul.

"Heaven is the delight of the heart, which is submerged in an ocean of love, in the very love of the most Holy Trinity. Heaven is family life in its perfection; it is the company of the angels and the saints; it is the presence of whatever is most pure, most innocent, most sweet, most holy. Heaven is life shared with our relatives and friends — the inexpressible tenderness of the most holy Virgin, our Mother; of Jesus, Friend, Brother, Spouse of our soul."

Think of everything on earth that irks us, saddens us, or torments our lives: nothing, nothing of that can follow us into heaven!

Think of everything that is best, everything that we desire here below without hope of ever obtaining it: we will enjoy it all in heaven in abundance and in intensity. And before long this happiness shall be ours for all eternity...!

We must state, however, that when the great masters of the human spirit try portraying for us the results of their deep contemplation — results which have to pass through the human mind and be translated into words — these become reduced, by comparison, to mere miserable stammering.

But, God be praised! Such weakness constitutes the best praise of beautiful paradise. There the vision of God will give us every happiness, every delight, every satisfaction, every joy; our souls will be immersed in a sea of delight and will enjoy a degree of happiness far greater than we could ever hope for.

In the sacred Scriptures we read that the Queen of Sheba went to Jerusalem in order to admire the wisdom and magnificence of King Solomon, of which she had heard people speak so much. Everything she saw at the court of the king was far beyond her expectations, and she had to admit that what she had heard approached only half the truth at best: "Happy are your men, happy these servants of yours, who stand before you always and listen to your wisdom" (1 Kgs. 10:8).

Similarly, those who go to heaven find a gladness far greater than they expect.

Oh, how beautiful heaven is! How delightful!

Let us imagine the most magnificent pageantry of nature, the most refined and beautiful artistic and aesthetic forms; let us imagine the softest music, the sweetest harmonies, the most melodious songs; let us also imagine the deepest and most intense joys the human heart can experience in the happiest moments of life: all these are but a very pale shadow in comparison with what is enjoyed in heaven. Regardless of all we may possibly imagine of beauty and delight in this life, we shall never be able to conceive with our limited minds the faintest idea of what heaven is really like.

Looking at his simple straw and wood hut, a poor mountaineer can never visualize what a royal palace looks like.

Inadequate and far from perfection, the following comparison made by some preachers in order to help people understand the delights of heaven has a certain beauty of expression. "Imagine," they say, "that a horse knew he was about to be given a banquet. What else would he expect but top-grade hay, a bag full of oats, or similar tasty fodder?" More or less, this brings out the restricted range of our mentality in attempting to picture the mysterious beauties of heaven. Accustomed as we are to the sight and enjoyment of earthly beauties, we suppose that those of heaven should be more or less of a similar nature. What a pity that we cannot even begin to imagine the nature of the good things in heaven our heavenly Father has reserved for those who love Him!

The Apostle St. Paul, who was transported into heaven while he was still living on earth, had to confess: "Eye has not seen, ear has not heard, nor has it so much as dawned on man what God has prepared for those who love him" (1 Cor. 2:9).

However, while we are waiting for the heavenly Father to call us home, let us follow the angels who ascended Jacob's mysterious ladder, which, while resting on earth, lost itself in the splendor of the heavens; sustained by an ardent faith, let us ascend to those mysterious and radiant regions where the very essence of God becomes visible to creatures.

We speak with the authority of those who were able to speak with knowledge—that is, on the word of the holy Apostles Paul and John.

The Two Seers

When on the island of Patmos, to which he had been exiled at the order of the Emperor Domitian, St. John experienced the marvelous visions he speaks of in the Apocalypse, or Book of Revelation.

And St. Paul writes: "I know a man in Christ who, fourteen years ago, whether he was in or outside his body I cannot say, only God can say—a man who was snatched up to the third heaven. I know that this man—whether in or outside his body I do not know, God knows—was snatched up to Paradise to hear words which cannot be uttered, words which no man may speak" (2 Cor. 12:2-3).

As if unable to say anything further about it, the Apostle sums up in a few words a story of priceless revelation.

Guided by these two New Testament seers, we proceed with our discussion about heaven.

The heaven to which St. Paul was raised is without doubt the true and proper heaven, the heaven of heavens, the place of perfect happiness promised by God to His faithful servants, the dear fatherland that gathers all the blessed into its radiant splendor. The mysterious words he spoke of must refer to the manifestation of the sacred humanity of our Lord Jesus Christ with the mysteries of His incarnation and death, of His glory in heaven, of the happiness of the saints, and of the magnificence of the royal palace of God!

O holy Apostle, why did you not at least describe those beauties that can be conceived of by our limited senses? No doubt you considered any attempt at description impossible, yet the exclamation of your soul: "I long to be freed from this life and to be with Christ" (Phil. 1:23) tells us much more than any other description; it fosters in our hearts the desire for heaven.

If it was impossible for the Apostle to speak of the things of heaven, he nevertheless pointed out the means of reaching that blessed goal: fulfillment of the precept of love toward God and neighbor.

It is wonderful to observe the identity of the means that the two seers recommend to us in order that we may become citizens of heaven — love.

In describing the visions he had at Patmos, St. John seems to make up for St. Paul's brevity. He uses an abundance of imagery and richness of expression. Although his account is rather obscure and mysterious, he hoped thus to satisfy in part the yearning of those who were not sufficiently satisfied with the brief portrayal given by St. Paul. But, alas! The boy digging in the sand and expecting to put all the water of the sea into the hole was not so far from succeeding as is one who presumes he can describe the mysterious heights of heaven.

Having seen in a vision the glorified hand of Jesus, St. Teresa of Avila remained in ecstasy for three days. Afterwards, she answered those who asked her to describe that hand by feebly comparing it with a shower of diamonds.

What can one say? Is it ever possible to reflect the measureless expanse of the universe in a fragment of mirror?

Having resolved to dictate a substantial description of heaven, St. Augustine wrote to St. Jerome to ask for advice. In the meantime, St. Jerome died, but in a dream the deceased appeared to his friend and said to him:

"Augustine, can you understand how one could possibly hold the entire earth in his grasp?"

"No."

"Can you at least understand how one could possibly gather all the waters of the seas and rivers in a small vase?"

"No."

"Then no one can ever describe how the infinite joy of God can be gathered into the heart of man."

Heaven is a marvel of divine power; it is as great and as infinite a good as God Himself. "I shall be your great reward!" He tells us.

One day the Lord granted St. Teresa of Avila the privilege of a peek through the gate of heaven. She wrote afterwards in her autobiography:

"The things I saw were so great and so marvelous that the smallest of them would be enough to dazzle a soul to its fullest capacity and to inspire it with the deepest scorn for the goods of this earthly life.

"No human spirit can conceive a fitting idea of them. This vision filled my soul with such happiness and intoxicated it with a joy so sweet that I cannot properly express it.

"While the Lord allowed me to admire such wonders, He told me: 'See, my daughter, what those who offend me lose.'"

Evidently the saint must have been immensely captivated, for the remainder of her life was one continuous pining for heaven.

Where she gives free reign to her unlimited yearning is in her canticles. We quote some stanzas of one of them. How majestic is its last verse, used as a refrain: "I die because I do not die."

How tedious is this life below,
This exile, with its grief and pains,
This dungeon and these cruel chains
In which the soul is forced to go!
Straining to leave this life of woe,
With anguish sharp and deep I cry:
"I die because I do not die."

How bitter our existence ere
We come at last the Lord to meet!

For, though the soul finds loving sweet,
The waiting-time is hard to bear.
O, from this leaden weight of care,
My God, relieve me speedily,
Who die because I do not die.

I only live because I know
That death's approach is very sure,
And hope is all the more secure
Since death and life together go.
O Death, thou life-creator, lo!
I wait upon thee, come thou nigh:
I die because I do not die.

That life, with life beyond recall,
Is truly life for evermore:
Until this present life be o'er.
We cannot savor life at all.
So, Death, retreat not at my call,
For life through death I can descry,
Who die because I do not die.

O life, what service can I pay
Unto my God who lives in me
Save if I first abandon thee
That I may merit thee for aye?
I'd win thee dying day by day,
Such yearning for my Spouse have I,
Dying because I do not die.

Then, Death, come pleasantly to me.
Come softly; undismay'd am I,
Who die because I do not die.

And in her life-long role of passionate lover of
God, she would go on repeating: "How long this exile
is, O Lord! How much more painful it is made by my
desire of seeing You! Lord, what can a soul do, shut

up in this prison? Oh, how long man's life is, although it is said to be short! Short it is, my God, to pass through it to gain the life that has no end, but very long for the soul that desires to see itself soon with You."

Similarly, our Lord showed a ray of heavenly glory to St. Catherine of Siena in one of her ecstasies. And when she came out of her rapture, she exclaimed: "I have seen marvelous things!... I have seen marvelous things!" Her confessor suggested that she describe more clearly what God had shown her, but she answered, "I would commit a grave error if I dared to do it; human words cannot express the beauty and the value of heavenly treasures."

Let us conclude with the words of St. Augustine: "The splendor of the eternal light is so great that if we were privileged to remain in it but a single day, we would despise for such a price numberless years full of delight and abundance of earthly goods. In heaven one possesses everything that he loves, and it would be impossible to desire more.

"In heaven there is only what is good, that is: the Infinite Good. God gives Himself to those who love Him, and for them the certainty of possessing and enjoying God forever is their supreme happiness."

The Mystic Rose of the Saints

In his thirtieth canto of "Paradise," Dante compares the light of glory, with which intelligent creatures see the Creator face to face, to a river of light that flows in an immense circle around the most Blessed Trinity. Arrayed on a gentle upward incline are all the souls of the blessed, positioned on more than a thousand circular steps ascending toward the center, whence all splendor is shed by the rays which God showers upon their assembly:

"Therefore in the form of an incandescent
  rose
The sainted hosts were pointed out to me —
That Christ in His Blood had espoused."

(Par. c. 31)

Meanwhile, angels winging gracefully about would momentarily alight upon the petals of that enormous flower and reascend, "up there where His love abides forever," like swarms of bees that now settle on the flowers to sip nectar and now return to the beehive.

In describing the loveliness of those angels, with faces radiant like glowing flames, with golden wings and bodies more iridescent than sunlit snow, the poet notes that in descending upon the rose they guided to his proper place each of the blessed entering the fatherland at last, and allotted to each that degree of light and love that he had earned during life in this land of exile.

O beautiful angels, when we shall arrive at the shores of heavenly bliss, assign us, too, a place in that mystic rose, so that feasting our eyes on that river of light, we may satisfy the thirst for truth and love we vainly try to quench now with the deficiency of the things of earth!

CHAPTER III

WHO GOES TO HEAVEN?

> *Who can ascend the mountain of the Lord?*
> *or who may stand in his holy place?*
> *He whose hands are sinless, whose heart is clean.*
>
> (Ps. 24:3-4)

Contemplation of the Heavens

How beautiful the skies are on a clear, bright, starry night!... The Big Dipper! the North Star!... Cassiopeia!... Venus!... Oh, how many stars and planets! Can it be true that those luminous points are many worlds rotating and revolving in space? And that the light of most of them, traveling at 186,000 miles per second, takes millions of years to reach us?

What astounding immensity! What unfathomable mystery!

Yet all this we shall understand, we shall penetrate one day...!

After the singing of matins, while his confreres went back to their cells, a young friar was struck by the glittering phenomenon of the skies over his head. He stopped, alone in the large cloister, and, while his eyes drank in that ocean of light and space, he thought: "That heaven is made for me.... I shall see all those stars one by one, I shall penetrate the unfathomable vastnesses which the astronomers are not able to measure.... I shall see God face to face; I

43

shall see my Mother Mary...the angels...St. Joseph, the holy Apostles Peter and Paul, the patriarchs, the prophets, the martyrs, the confessors, the virgins.... They all will live with me and will be my friends and companions.... There the gay liveliness of Agnes, the smiling sweetness of Teresa, the gay harmonies of Cecilia will delight my senses. I, myself, by a mysterious uplift of my faculties, shall enjoy the gift of a musician who creates indescribable melodies.... I shall taste the ecstasies Raphael and Michelangelo tasted as they looked upon the wonders their brushes produced. The rapture of the poet who sings his luminous visions!... What joy, what gaiety, what happiness!

"I shall meet my mother, my father, my grandparents, brothers, and relatives.... How heartily I shall embrace my mother! After having been separated, how happy shall we be, nevermore to be apart, nevermore! Always gay, always joyous, always happy!

"I shall share the glory that my Mother Mary received on the day she was assumed into heaven; the embrace she gave her divine Son, who crowned her Queen and Lady of all that He created...."

Here the friar interrupted his soliloquy: "But why do I speak only of myself?...and only to myself?..."

Yes, you are right, O young cloistered one, who have inscribed on the door of your cell: "From here you shall go to heaven." Heaven is not for you alone; the life of every man is a road that leads to eternity. Men's eyes are fixed on the blessed fatherland; eternity is the point of orientation for their existence.

In her "Story of a Soul," St. Thérèse of the Child Jesus relates that her aunt used to invite her and her sisters, one at a time, to spend the evening at her home. Thérèse confesses that she was very happy when her turn came.

"At about eight o'clock Papa would come to bring me home, and I remember how on the way I would look with great delight up at the stars. Orion's belt, like a cluster of diamonds, hung in the deep vault overhead and had a wonderful fascination for me because I saw in it a likeness to the letter T. 'Look, Papa!' I would cry, 'my name is written in heaven!' Then, oblivious of my dull, earthly surroundings, I would ask him to lead me on, while with head thrown back, I would gaze untiringly at the starry skies."

If we tried to give our souls the attitude of complete abandonment to God that little Thérèse had when she was led home by her father, we, too, could say that we see our names written in heaven.

The starry sky always has mysterious attractions for the pure of heart; each reads his name in it.

Who Goes to Heaven?

Whoever wants to go there. "Before man are life and death, whichever he chooses shall be given him" (Sir. 15:17).

God wants us all to be saved. St. Paul says: "This is the will of God, your sanctification" (cf. 1 Thes. 4:3). God wants us not only to be saved, but to attain sanctity.

However, He does not act alone in working out our sanctification. He certainly does the most; He leaves the least for us to do, in order to give us the merit of our free cooperation. Thus the Supreme Judge may give us heaven as our reward. "God, who has created you without your cooperation," declares St. Augustine, "will not save you without your cooperation." Therefore, only he who exerts this minimum of cooperation with God's work will go to heaven.

The hope of reaching heaven is open to everybody; every man of good will can reach the kingdom of everlasting happiness.

D. A. Coiazzi wrote significantly: "One spring morning two little birds went to build their nests. One of them found a tree and built its nest in its branches. It was a delightful location indeed: flowers filled the air with their fragrance; at the foot of the tree a sparkling brook reflected the sun during the day, and the starry sky at night. But one night there was a terrible storm and the brook became a raging torrent. It flooded the land bordering it and uprooted the nearby trees. The tree in whose branches the bird had built its nest was also carried off, and the little nest destroyed.

"That little bird had provided only for clear days and calm nights. The other bird had built its nest in a crevice among the rocks of an old cliff. The nest was agog with excitement, for the storm that had wrought havoc in the valley blew around the cliff, too, but it was not able to move the nest.

"The next day the sun shone again; the bird's nest was safe."

And what of us? Where do we build our spiritual structure? Do we construct it among the weak branches of purely human friendship, in the pleasing valley of life, by the brook of worldly pleasures where the blossoms of self-indulgence give off delicious perfumes, or do we build it among the solid rocks, the cliff of the ages? Do we build only for clear days or also for floods and storms? What people go to heaven? Those who take care that their building be not shattered on stormy days, who do not let the ups and downs of life discourage them, who uplift themselves through prayer and resign themselves to God's will when the day of trial comes—in short, those who keep looking heavenward, breathing an atmosphere entirely of faith, of purity, of trust in God; those who sing, with the life they daily live, that admirable hymn which the Eagle of Carmel, Teresa of Jesus, kept as a bookmark in her breviary:

> Let nothing disturb thee,
> Nothing affright thee;
> All things are passing;
> God never changeth.
> Patience overcomes all things;
> He who possesses God
> Lacks nothing;
> God alone sufficeth.

The Value of Life

A fundamental question in the catechism is: "Why did God make you?"

The answer is definite: "God made me to know Him, to love Him, and to serve Him in this world and to be happy with Him forever in heaven."

Nothing is more important than knowing the ultimate end of life—an end for which we must strive with all our might.

It is sad to see that so many persons spend their lives working and studying for some indifferent end, showing no interest in learning why they are in this world, where they came from, and where they are going.

Some declare that we are in this world to enjoy life.

What can entirely satisfy the human heart? Not wealth, indeed, since so few succeed in acquiring it; not honors; not science; and certainly not mere sensual pleasures.

When anything does not serve its purpose, we throw it away; if life were made merely to be enjoyed, nothing would remain but to cut it short, since it brings us more pain than real pleasure. The true and only pleasure that satisfies our hearts in this life is to live by doing the will of God and by seeking peace and tranquility of conscience, which are sure tokens of eternal happiness.

The true value of life is a problem that vexes man at all times; and yet, unfortunately, in our enlightened times the simple solution is rejected, by some, even with horror.

Remarkably to the point is an article written by Cardinal Maffi after an unfortunate professor named Ardigo attempted to commit suicide. At the age of ninety, Ardigo had not yet learned the value of life and tried to end it, repeating over and over: "Of what use is life? Let me die."

"It is strange," wrote Cardinal Maffi, with the heart of a shepherd and father. "The soft, white light of the friendly lamp nearby shines on the pages he sweats over. The pen drinks profusely of the ink in the inkstand and then runs, docile and swift, under the impulse of his hand and leaves its imprint on the paper. The philosopher knows what use to him are the lamp, the inkstand, the pen, his hand, and the paper. Yet, he does not know of what use his own life is to him!

"Do cold, heat, and the need of rest bother him? He puts on or takes off some of his clothes, adjusts the window shutters for the right amount of air and sun, sits down to a meal that will nourish him sufficiently. The philosopher knows how clothes, food, and house help him keep, protect, and sustain life.

"He knows that night is made for rest, and day for work; that vacations serve to renew one's energy; that the scholastic year is for studies; childhood, for growing; youth, to gain an education and culture....

"He knows the purpose of every phase and time of life: he does not know, however, the aim of life, whole and entire! He knows the use of everything around him; yet he does not know of what use he himself is! He knows that a razor may be used to end life; he does not know the value, the why, the reason of the life that is destroyed. And this after more than fifty years of teaching, after ninety years of life!

"He asks to be allowed to drown in his own blood his life as something annoying, useless, cumbersome, because he does not know of what use it is!"

Two years later the unfortunate professor succeeded in doing away with himself.

What is the purpose of life?

To earn heaven.

The very moment we lose sight of this fundamental truth, we are shipwrecked.

Life is a trial and heaven is the reward.

Life is a brief and unavoidable trial on which depends an eternity of delight or of torment.

Death is the termination and crown of this trial of fidelity: "Cleverly done! You too are an industrious and reliable servant.... Come, share your master's joy!" (Mt. 25:23)

What is the purpose of life? To earn us a happy eternity: "The present burden of our trial is light enough, and earns for us an eternal weight of glory beyond all comparison" (2 Cor. 4:17).

But in order that all the deeds in life be reflected and fixed in the blessed eternity, it is necessary to work for heaven.

Marveling at the absolute dedication of missionaries working among the lepers, a doctor told one of the sisters that he wouldn't do what she was doing for a million dollars.

"Neither would I," she replied, "but for God and heaven I'll do this and even more."

Are all good works destined for heaven?

No, not all of them: only those which bear the stamp of eternity — those that are directed to heaven, to God.

A story is told about a Polish nobleman who was very generous in good works to the point of making great financial sacrifices. In his old age, he had the following dream: "It seemed that I had been taken up to a high region extraordinarily beautiful and unfamiliar. There I saw great numbers of heavenly figures who seemed absorbed in writing with great earnestness.

"I approached one of these beings and asked what they were writing down with such eagerness.

"He answered me most kindly: 'We are the angels of God, and we write here, in these pages of the book of life, the good deeds of the men who are on earth.'

"This answer stimulated my curiosity, and wishing to know how I stood in regard to merits for eternity, I whispered to the angel: 'May I see what is recorded on my page?'

"'Why not?' he answered. And he looked for my page and handed it to me.

"Imagine my astonishment, or to be more exact, imagine my fear when I found that, except for a few lines, the page was blank.

"'Is it possible that until now I have no merits for eternal life?' I exclaimed. 'I have done so many good deeds, and have made great sacrifices!'

"The present burden of our trial
is light enough, and earns for us
an eternal weight of glory
beyond all comparison."

—2 Cor. 4:17

"'My friend,' the angel answered, 'here in these pages that make up the book of life are recorded only those things which men do *for God* and *for the love of God.*'"

Everyone in this world works and makes efforts, but how many will have pages written in the book of life?

How many work for heaven?

Charity, the holy love of God, is the magic wand that turns whatever it touches into gold. Touching our thoughts, our labors, our sorrows—our entire life—charity makes everything golden, that is, meritorious for everlasting life.

To the question, "Who deserves heaven?" the catechism answers: "He who is good deserves heaven, that is, he who loves and faithfully serves God and dies in His grace."

Therefore, all those who have loved and served God in this life and then die in His grace, go to heaven.

One day St. Francis de Sales met a bricklayer, and asked: "What are you building, brother?"

"Walls, from morning to night."

"Why do you build walls?"

"Oh, that's a good one! To earn money, of course."

"And why do you want to earn money?"

"To buy bread."

"Why so?"

"So that I may live."

"And, for what do you live?"

At this point the bricklayer became confused and could not find an answer, just as it would happen to millions of other men. St. Francis, on the other hand, suggested the right answer, by reminding him that the ultimate purpose of man is: "to work for God in order to enjoy Him for all eternity."

Who Has a Right to Heaven?

Not long ago a certain priest received a letter which read: "It is pitiful to see the poor men and women who tell you with painful resignation, 'Heaven is not for us!' According to their way of thinking, heaven is only for men and women in religion; for those who do good deeds; above all, for children who die soon after having received Baptism; and, some say, for people well known for their holiness."

These poor people are resigned to not going to heaven as they are resigned to not being rich. Such seems to be the destiny of the poor — to be unhappy both in this world and in the next. This is incredible, and yet I have been assured that among the good such a spiritual disease, such a fatalism, is common. No, heaven is for everyone and especially for the humble, for those who labor and suffer with faith.

It is for the poor — men, women and children alike — for farmers, for laborers, for everyone. Do you want to be convinced? Recall the great throng that followed the Divine Master from city to city, from village to village, and from desert to desert. Twice our Lord was obliged to multiply loaves for them. Who were they? Certainly not the rich and powerful, not the great capitalists, the great land-owners. They were the poor, the humble — peasants, sinners, derelicts, people who suffered and wept. For them the Divine Master preached the beatitudes; about them He was concerned in a special way. And furthermore, it was from among them that He chose His apostles.

What cause for rejoicing have the humble, for whom this earth truly is a valley of tears!

"How happy are the poor in spirit.... Happy those who mourn.... Happy those who hunger and thirst for what is right...theirs is the kingdom of heaven" (Mt. 5:3, 5, 6, 10) (JB).

The Words of the Divine Master

"Seeing the crowds, he went up the hill. There he sat down and was joined by his disciples. Then he began to speak. This is what he taught them:

'How happy are the poor in spirit;
theirs is the kingdom of heaven.
Happy the gentle:
they shall have the earth for their heritage.
Happy those who mourn:
they shall be comforted.
Happy those who hunger and thirst for what is right:
they shall be satisfied.
Happy the merciful:
they shall have mercy shown them.
Happy the pure in heart:
they shall see God.
Happy the peacemakers:
they shall be called sons of God.
Happy those who are persecuted in the cause of right:
theirs is the kingdom of heaven.

'Happy are you when people abuse you and persecute you and speak all kinds of calumny against you on my account. Rejoice and be glad, for your reward will be great in heaven; this is how they persecuted the prophets before you!'" (Mt. 5:1-12) (JB)

Here is the real moral of the Gospel. To those who seek riches, Jesus holds out the joys that can come from a life of poverty. To the aggressive and power-hungry, He extends the way of meekness and humility. To the greedy for pleasure, He offers the soothing balm of tears. To those who hunger and thirst, He proposes the nourishment of justice. To souls without mercy, He teaches mercy and pardon. To the sensual, He holds out the attraction of purity. To those who chafe under the yoke, He grants the joy of the peaceful and of the persecuted.

What disillusionment—especially for the powerful of the world!

Yet, nowadays, how many really understand the teaching of the Divine Master?

The entirely human conception that the Jewish people had of the Messiah prevented them from penetrating the real significance of the messianic prophecies, of which they understood only the literal sense, not the spirit.

The sad inclination of fallen human nature that caused the misunderstanding of the Jews is still today a formidable obstacle to the understanding of the teachings of the Divine Master. For the majority of men, the preoccupations of this world dominate everything, absorb all other activities, corrupt the mind, distract from prayer, and at times even alienate one from religion itself. When nothing else is sought but riches, pleasures and honors, the sense of the kingdom of God is lost.

In order that the thought of this supernatural kingdom may become a strategic influence in the arena of life, we need the supernatural help of grace. Without the light of divine grace, the admirable teaching of the beatitudes passes over our heads, flashes with a momentary influence like a luminous meteor, then sinks to oblivion in the indifferent intellect.

The foundations on which the kingdom of God must rest are poverty, humility and tears. Humility, poverty and affliction snatch man from the domination of his fallen nature and let peace, purity and charity — sweet images of the kingdom of God — reign in his soul. Let us not concentrate our attention on the coarse shallowness of a cynical and deceiving world, nor on tinsel riches, which constitute a great danger to the soul.

St. Paul writes to his disciple Timothy: "Tell those who are rich in this world's goods not to be proud, and not to rely on so uncertain a thing as wealth. Let them trust in the God who provides us richly with all things for our use. Charge them to do good, to be rich in good works and generous, sharing what they have. Thus will they build a secure foundation for the future, for receiving that life which is life indeed" (1 Tm. 6:17-19).

Let us learn how to battle temptation with true Christian character, to conquer evil with virtue, to be living witnesses to the honor and glory of God.

The Two Roads

Two roads lead to heaven: the road of innocence and the road of penance. Children who die after Baptism and souls who have never committed mortal sin enter heaven by the road of innocence. The road of penance is for everyone who has sinned mortally after Baptism, but has washed his sins in a double bath — that of his own tears and that of the blood of Jesus. This second road is the one through which the vast majority of Christians are saved. We who so many times have been shipwrecked in the sea of life can hope to reach heaven only by holding fast to this plank of salvation. Augustine and Mary of Magdala arrived by this road and now occupy that lofty place from which they shed radiance upon all mankind. A great number of confessors who reached heaven through this second road bear witness to the infinite goodness of God, to the infinite mercy of Jesus, who shed His blood for them. Blessed be the sacrament of Penance, born of the Heart of God and poured forth from His open side!

"I absolve you!" said in the sacrament of reconciliation is the divine formula that restores peace to souls and gives to us weak human creatures a visible sign of pardon and, hence, of eternal salvation.

In Spain, veneration is given to a crucifix that has one arm unfastened and hanging down along the body. It is said that one day, with much sorrow, a great sinner was making his confession to a priest beneath this crucifix. The confessor was uncertain as to whether he should absolve the sinner, for the sins were so grievous!

The sinner pleaded...and finally the confessor said: "All right. I'll absolve you this time, but you must not fall again."

But the sinner was very weak and soon fell again.

Repentance brought him back to the feet of the crucifix. "No," the confessor said, "this time I will not absolve you." But the penitent begged and wept until the confessor was moved to pity and again sent him away absolved.

A longer period of time went by; the sinner fell again. "This is enough," said the priest. "Your repentance is not sincere."

"Yes, Father, I am sincere, only I'm too weak. Help me. My soul is so sick!"

"No. There is no more pardon for you."

At this terrible judgment, the sinner sank to the ground in grief.

Suddenly a heartrending sob came from the crucifix. By the dim light Christ could be seen to lift His unfastened right hand and trace the sign of absolution over the sinner's head as He said: "You do not pardon because you have not shed all your blood for him."

Why should not the sinner hope for heaven from the moment that Jesus Christ came down on earth to reconcile man with God?

To make us understand His love for men and His divine will to save them, Jesus has told us the parables of the prodigal son, of the lost sheep, and of the lost coin. He Himself appears in these parables as the aged father who with indescribable joy embraces the son returning repentant to him, as the shepherd in search of the senseless little lamb that has strayed away from the fold, as the woman who, after prolonged search, feels the urge of sharing with her friends the joy of having found the coin which she had considered lost forever.

During His life on earth, the divine Savior went in search of sinners and offered them salvation. He granted pardon to whosoever asked for it. He forgave Magdalene, the good thief, Zaccheus, and Peter. With divine generosity, He forgives all those who approach Him with a penitent heart and are willing to change their way of life.

After he had obtained the "Portiuncula" indulgence from the Pope, St. Francis of Assisi went about shouting: "Everyone in heaven! Everyone in heaven!" And he invited the people to enter his quaint little church.

Yes, all to heaven, since:

"Infinite Goodness has such wide arms
To enfold in them all who turn to it."

(Purg. c. 3, 122-123)

Mixed with the blood of Jesus in the sacrament of Penance, a tear of repentance from us is enough to obtain justification. If, unfortunately, we should be in a state of sin, let us immediately run to God, and cast ourselves upon His mercy.

"At last I admitted to you I had sinned;
no longer concealing my guilt....
And you, you have forgiven the wrong I did,
have pardoned my sin" (Ps. 32:5) (JB).

Blessed Are They

In his Apocalypse, or Book of Revelation, St. John testifies to having seen blessed spirits with censors and golden cups full of perfume, from which a most delightful fragrance rose to the throne of the Most High. These were the prayers and sufferings of the just, still living on earth (cf. Rv. 5).

An angel noticed the amazement of John, as he contemplated that great multitude "which no man could number." When asked by him who they were and where they came from, the angel enlightened him by replying: "These are the ones who have survived the great period of trial" (Rv. 7:14).

Wax has to be subjected to heat in order to receive the mark of a seal; so, too, man, in order to be marked with the imprint of heavenly glory, must pass through the fires of tribulation. "I was sent to put you to the test" (Tb. 12:14). Often sufferings are a sign of God's love: "Those whom I love I rebuke and chastise" (Rv. 3:19). Therefore, they also are a sign of predestination, a pledge of future glory.

Blessed is the man who is tried by God! Burdened with difficult trials and terrible temptations, the Apostle St. Paul begged the Lord to free him from them, but God answered: "My grace is enough for you, for in weakness power reaches perfection." And so, Paul wrote, "I willingly boast of my weaknesses instead, that the power of Christ may rest upon me. Therefore I am content with weakness, with mistreatment, with distress, with persecutions and difficulties for the sake of Christ; for when I am powerless, it is then that I am strong" (2 Cor. 12:9-10).

Who better than Jesus knew what was more beneficial to man for him to attain eternal happiness? Among the beatitudes there is not even one which says: "Blessed are the rich, blessed are those who have good times, blessed are the prominent in the world." Rather, they proclaim: "How blest are the poor; blest are the lowly; blest are the single-hearted; blest too are the sorrowing; blest are those persecuted for holiness' sake" (Mt. 5:3-10). Why so? Because they will have a just reward, not in this life but in the life to come.

To the apostles who asked what their reward would be for having abandoned everything to follow Him, Jesus answered: "everyone who has given up home, brothers or sisters, father or mother, wife or children or property for my sake will receive many times as much and inherit everlasting life" (Mt. 19:29). Besides, He proclaims: "If anyone wants to be a follower of mine, let him renounce himself and take up his cross and follow me" (Mt. 16:24) (JB).

Trials are means of keeping us in the state of grace and virtue, of calling us back or preserving us from sin and hell, and of securing life everlasting.

Not only with resignation but also with thankful-
ness let us accept all the trials that our Lord is pleased
to send us, since He is the God who "casts us down
and revives us, who afflicts and comforts us" (Man-
zoni).

Before the light of revelation came to illumine
men's minds, it was believed, even by the good,
that misfortunes were always signs of punishment
for sin committed. The entire book of Job is related
to this important question. Even the apostles seemed
to have been of the same mentality. Concerning the
affliction of the man born blind, they asked the
Master whether the man or his parents had sinned.
Evidently they were not as yet imbued with the
science of the cross. Only after the tragedy of Calvary
did they understand: "Did not the Messiah have to
undergo all this so as to enter into his glory?" (Lk.
24:26)

The cross! There we have it—the royal road to
heaven!

The saints knew this when they would exclaim:
"Either·suffering or death"; "I die because I do not
die"; "To suffer and not to die"; "To suffer and be
despised for you."

"The more you are tried, the more you enrich
yourself," the saintly Abbot of Clairvaux used to
say.

After all, "by turning everything to their good
God cooperates with all those who love him" (Rom.
8:28) (JB).

In every kind of trial, the Christian must say to
himself, "I am sure that poverty, sickness, persecutions, calumnies, exile and death are regulated be-
forehand by the fatherly, infinite goodness of divine
Providence, to prepare the way to the future reward."

In humble submission, he prays: "Our Father, who art in heaven, hallowed be Thy name; Thy kingdom come, Thy will be done...."

Therefore, trials, patiently endured, constitute the gate to heaven. Holy Scripture teaches us this: "Did not the Messiah have to undergo all this so as to enter into his glory?" (Lk. 24:26); and again: "We must undergo many trials if we are to enter into the reign of God" (Acts 14:21).

Now, if Jesus Christ, our Lord, had to suffer all sorts of tribulations to enter into His glory, we, members of His Mystical Body, must also travel the same road of suffering and carry the same cross; there is no other road to heaven. For confirmation of this, let us consider the lives of the saints! See how the majority of them had no wealth on earth other than the riches of the cross, the grace of God, and the hope of heaven.

The cross—the royal road to heaven.

PART II

OUR BLESSED HOMELAND

And all shall sing, in their festive dance:
"My home is within you."

(Ps. 87:7)

CHAPTER I

THE INHERITANCE OF THE ELECT

Heavenly Jerusalem, a blessed vision of peace!

A Prophetic Vision

In one of the visions he had on the island of Patmos, the Apostle St. John described the heavenly Jerusalem, or paradise, thus:

"One of the seven angels that had the seven bowls full of the seven last plagues came to speak to me, and said, 'Come here and I will show you the bride that the Lamb has married.' In the spirit, he took me to the top of an enormous high mountain, and showed me Jerusalem, the holy city, coming down from God out of heaven. It had all the radiant glory of God and glittered like some precious jewel òf crystal-clear diamond. The walls of it were of a great height, and had twelve gates; at each of the twelve gates there was an angel, and over the gates were written the names of the twelve tribes of Israel; on the east there were three gates, on the north three gates, on the south three gates, and on the west three gates. The city walls stood on twelve foundation stones, each one of which bore the name of one of the twelve apostles of the Lamb.

"The angel that was speaking to me was carrying a gold measuring rod to measure the city and its gates and wall. The plan of the city is perfectly square, its length the same as its breadth. He measured the city with his rod and it was twelve thousand furlongs in length and in breadth, and equal in height. He measured its wall, and this was a hundred and forty-four cubits high — the angel was using the ordinary cubit. The wall was built of diamond, and the city of pure gold, like polished glass. The foundations of the city wall were faced with all kinds of precious stone: the first with diamond, the second lapis lazuli, the third turquoise, the fourth crystal, the fifth agate, the sixth ruby, the seventh gold quartz, the eighth malachite, the ninth topaz, the tenth emerald, the eleventh sapphire and the twelfth amethyst. The twelve gates were twelve pearls, each gate being made of a single pearl, and the main street of the city was pure gold, transparent as glass. I saw that there was no temple in the city since the Lord God Almighty and the Lamb were themselves the temple, and the city did not need the sun or the moon for light, since it was lit by the radiant glory of God and the Lamb was a lighted torch for it. The pagan nations will live by its light and the kings of the earth will bring it their treasures. The gates of it will never be shut by day — and there will be no night there — and the nations will come, bringing their treasure and their wealth. Nothing unclean may come into it: no one who does what is loathsome or false, but only those who are listed in the Lamb's book of life" (Rv. 21:9-27) (JB).

It is evident that this description cannot be understood by our limited imaginations; its true meaning is too mysterious and spiritual. The delights and beauties of heaven infinitely surpass all that the human mind can imagine or the human tongue express.

Whatever we can imagine of the most marvelous and sublime is no more than the most pale impression from which we can but imperfectly picture the radiance of the city of God, where our Lord dwells in luminous resplendence that is beyond description.

"Glorious things are said of you, O city of God," (Ps. 87:3) the psalmist exclaims. "How lovely is your dwelling place, O Lord of hosts! My soul yearns and pines for the courts of the Lord" (Ps. 84:2-3).

Immersed in the same contemplation, a prophet declares: "O Israel, how vast is the house of God, how broad the scope of his dominion: Vast and endless, high and immeasurable!" (Bar. 3:24-25)

The author of *The Year With God* sums up these magnificent concepts in one paragraph: "Who can ever make us understand the happiness of the saints? Everything that God has created in the universe — the marvels of the earth, the sea, the skies — cannot give the faintest idea of the beauty and magnificence of the heavenly dwelling. To compare that abode to the palaces of kings, to the splendid temple of Solomon, is like comparing the work of men with that of God. To state that it is a city of princes, a Jerusalem with diamond gates and with walls of precious stones seems to contradict the Apostle, who declares that man's eyes have never seen, nor ears heard, nor heart conceived what God has prepared for those who love Him. 'There,' says St. John, 'there is neither pain nor tears, nor sufferings; no change of day or night, of warmth or cold, of health or sickness, of joys or afflictions.'

"Everything in that delightful kingdom is ever in harmony with the wishes of those who possess it.... Immersed in an ocean of divine joy, they share in God's own happiness."

Entranced by the beauties of heaven and intensely eager to possess them, St. Augustine wrote: "O wonderful home, O enchanting palace sparkling with heavenly light, how enraptured I am by your beauty, which fears no comparison — blessed abode of the glory of my God, who made it and dwells within it!

"Sinners may possess the earth and be blinded by the clouds of indifference they raise. As for myself, I prefer to retire into the quiet of my little room, where I may sing canticles of love in the ardor of my burning passion for your beauty! There, too, with unutterable sighs, I may bemoan the misery of my earthly pilgrimage and lift up my heart to the heavenly Jerusalem, which is my fatherland...toward which rise the fondest hopes of my soul."

And yet, streets paved with transparent gold, walls built of crystal and adorned with precious stones count for little when compared with the sublime thoughts that the Holy Spirit has revealed to us: that is, this heavenly city of God consists of all the riches and treasures of divine mercy, and its most magnificent splendor is the justice and truth of God.

Our true heaven in the city of the blessed will be knowing, loving, possessing and enjoying God, Infinite Beauty, Eternal Truth, Supreme Good.

"O joy supreme, unspoken delectation!
O lasting life of love and peace veracious!
O safest, most unhungered domination!"

(Par. c. 27, 7-9)

But how can we grasp these truths?

Poor pilgrims that we are, on this earth of exile, "away from the Lord" (2 Cor. 5:6), our feeble reason is capable of only the palest of imaginings.

Even Plotinus, the pagan philosopher, goes so far as to say that the vision of God is of such sublime beauty and worthy of such love that without it even a man who possesses an abundance of all other goods is still a most unhappy being.

Monsabre writes this about heaven: "It is a state in which the world, purified and wrapped in new splendors, better reflects the divine perfections and reveals to us secrets of grandeur, of wisdom, and of love that we could not possibly have discovered in this mortal life; a state in which the soul, freer from the shadows of the flesh than it was here below, sees better, in the clearer light of its faculties, the radiations of eternal beauty; a state in which the body, freed from every weakness, satisfied in its legitimate desires, submits, without resistance and without effort, to the magnetism of a superior life."

But is all this heaven?

No, it is still merely a shadow—merely a distantly vague figure.

In vain do artists try to reproduce heaven's beauties on canvas; in vain do poets translate their glowing concepts into verses; in vain do theologians attempt to formulate definitions and the mystics try, with all their heart and soul, to explain them through comparisons. All, all, is in vain.

Something can be understood, however, by observing the behavior of those who have been fortunate enough to be given a foretaste of heaven or who have perceived its beauties through divine grace.

After an adventurous youth, St. Jerome Emiliani dedicated himself entirely to works of mercy and penance. It was his custom to withdraw to a cave near his orphanage at Somasca, Italy, and spend his time in contemplation. Up there, between heaven and earth, where the noise of the world could not reach—there, nearer to God, Jerome experienced heavenly ecstasies.

Nowadays, a staircase called the "Scala Santa," leads up to the cave. It consists of large stone steps. But back then, one had to toil his way among bushes and steep bluffs. Up there the saint spent the best days of his long and hard life in continuous prayer and communication with God. His little orphans said that sometimes they would see him come out of that thorny wilderness transfigured, a grave and serene tenderness in his face. His eyes were luminous and from his person shone something indefinable which conquered hearts, as generally happens when one comes in contact with the supernatural.

They used to compare him to Moses coming down from Mount Sinai with his face aglow.

Such transformations are found also in the lives of other saints, particularly the ecstatics: St. Gertrude, St. Teresa, St. Mary Magdalene de Pazzi....

Enlightened by the Holy Spirit, the Church sings:

Jerusalem, O city blest!
Dear vision of celestial rest!
Which, far above the starry sky,
Piled up with living stones on high,
Your gates a pearly lustre pour:
Your gates are open evermore;
And thither evermore draw nigh
All who for Christ have dared to die;
Or driven by love for their dear Lord,
Have pains endured, and joys abhorred.
You, too, O Church, which here we see,
Have not been built up easily.

...Long worked the head and toiled the hand,
Ere stood thy stones as now they stand.

This hymn is an admirable paraphrase of the words of St. Paul in his letter to the Ephesians: "This means that you are strangers and aliens no longer. No, you are fellow citizens of the saints and members of the household of God. You form a building which rises on the foundation of the apostles and prophets, with Christ Jesus himself as the capstone. Through him the whole structure is fitted together and takes shape as a holy temple in the Lord; in him you are being built into this temple, to become a dwelling place for God in the Spirit" (Eph. 2:19-22).

Therefore, each one of us is a pebble shaped by the sanctifying action of the Holy Spirit, according to the pattern that is in the mind of God, to be set in this mystic structure.

The events of life, its joys and sorrows, its consolations and troubles, all work together wisely to give form and particular splendor to that precious stone which becomes the prized possession and glory of each of the blessed elect in heaven.

The Most Beautiful Adornment of Heaven

After having described the mystical rose of the saints, Dante says:

"I raised my eyes, and as when morn is lining
The eastern brim of the horizon's fountain,
It far surpasses that of sun declining—
Thus, as from vale ascending into mountain,
My eyes beheld, on farthest margin raining,
A light which far surpassed all other fountain."
(Par. c. 31, 118-123)

And towards that radiance he saw numberless angels converging with spread wings.

What was it?

It was the throne of Mary, the Queen of Heaven, who responded with a smile to the joyous expressions of the angels and saints.

> "...What delight she was in the eyes of all the other saints."
>
> (Par. c. 31, 134-135)

It is certainly not easy to describe what Mary is to the blessed in heaven. Even Dante, with all the skill of his intellect, scarcely presumes to attempt it:

> "And though my trumpet notes could equal, blowing,
> Power to imagine — still they had not earned
> Title the least to tell joys from her flowing."
>
> (Par. c. 31, 136-138)

The fathers of the Church say that Mary, by herself alone, forms a heaven for the blessed. As the dearly beloved daughter of the Father, Mother of the divine Son, and bride of the Holy Spirit, she is the most beautiful canticle, the most harmonious note, the brightest light in that indescribable celebration of heaven. Her most pure body is more resplendent than the heavenly spirits themselves, and this spotlessness of hers represents the victory of God over human flesh.

"As the light of the sun surpasses the splendor of the stars," St. Basil writes, "so the glory of the Mother of God surpasses that of all the other blessed."

St. Peter Damian adds: "As the stars and the moon disappear, so to speak, at the rising of the sun, so the heavenly light of the angels and saints is almost eclipsed by the splendor of Mary."

"The souls of the virtuous
are in the hands of God,
no torment shall ever touch them."
—Wisdom 3:1 (JB)

"As the moon and the planets reflect the light of the sun, so the blessed experience an increase in happiness and joy because of the vision and reflection of the glory of Mary," concludes St. Bernardine.

In the Apocalypse, or Book of Revelation, St. John describes a great wonder in heaven: "...a woman clothed with the sun, with the moon under her feet, and on her head a crown of twelve stars" (Rv. 12:1).

But how inadequate an image this description must be in comparison with reality! The crown which the Most Holy Trinity has placed on Mary's head is immensely more resplendent than a crown of shining stars. The light of day is gloomy darkness in comparison with the Sun of Justice by whose rays Mary is encompassed; and for a footstool at her feet, heavenly spirits entwine themselves in place of the moon.

All the Church triumphant sings to you, O Mary, who, although a creature born to man on earth, sit as Queen in the glory which surrounds the infinite majesty of God in heaven. The blessed venerate you because you are the glory of the heavenly Jerusalem, the delight of the people of God, the honor of humanity united in triumph to the Lord Jesus Christ.

MAN'S PERFECT HAPPINESS

> They have their fill of the prime gifts
> of your house;
> from your delightful stream you give
> them to drink.
>
> (Ps. 36:9)

Eternal Joy

Sacred Scripture contains a wonderful text with which it describes the mysterious happiness of the just:

"...the souls of the virtuous are in the hands of God, no torment shall ever touch them.
In the eyes of the unwise, they did appear to die, their going looked like a disaster,
their leaving us, like annihilation;
but they are in peace.
If they experienced punishment as men see it, their hope was rich with immortality;
slight was their affliction, great will their blessings be.
God has put them to the test
and proved them worthy to be with him;
he has tested them like gold in a furnace,
and accepted them as a holocaust.
When the time comes for his visitation they will shine out;
as sparks run through the stubble, so will they.
They shall judge nations, rule over peoples,
and the Lord will be their king for ever.
They who trust in him will understand the truth,

those who are faithful will live with him in love; for grace and mercy await those he has chosen" (Wis. 3:1-9) (JB).

"Therefore shall they receive the splendid crown, the beauteous diadem, from the hand of the Lord— For he shall shelter them with his right hand, and protect them with his arm" (Wis. 5:16).

In Psalm 36, the royal prophet says of God: "from your delightful stream you give them to drink" (Ps. 36:9).

St. Anselm compares these pleasures to an ocean: "As a fish is entirely surrounded by water in the sea, so the soul of the just will be immersed in the joy of God: joy internally, joy externally—deep joy, sublime joy, omnipresent joy."

The soul will see God, will possess Him, will enjoy Him—and in this consists the essence of bliss.

St. Bernard once was given the opportunity of enjoying God. Speaking of it later on, he exclaimed, "Oh, would that I again had the chance of enjoying You, O Lord, at the price of a thousand deaths!"

And he added: "If the pleasure of the soul is so great when only a drop of heavenly bliss comes to pervade it, what will it be like in heaven, where the joy and happiness of God will inundate us like a river?"

The mind of man passionately seeks truth, just as his heart passionately seeks love. This thirst for truth can be quenched only in heaven.

The sight of Eternal Truth will be such a joy that all the sense pleasures of man cannot even begin to compare with it.

St. Augustine wrote: "As long as my heart was in the abyss of sin, I thirsted for truth but was not sure I could find it. Only through Jesus Christ have

I found grace and truth. And its full light, which lasts forever and never diminishes for us, will shine only in heaven, where joy in God, who is Truth, will be eternal, blessed life."

What is human knowledge before the majesty of God and His eternal attributes? "Every just man," says St. Anselm, "will possess in heaven such knowledge that nothing which he wishes to know will remain unknown to him, neither of the past nor of the future." Thrusting his gaze into the divinity, he will be filled with complete, heavenly wisdom. The mysteries of creation, of the redemption, of divine Providence, of sanctification, of the government of the world and of souls, will be laid bare to us. All our existence will be displayed before our eyes. Then we will see how everything came about for our own greatest good. We will understand the reason for mysterious facts that we desire to unveil.

However, we shall have to stop short of Him who dwells in light inaccessible, "whom no human being has ever seen or can see" (1 Tm. 6:16). Only Jesus Christ, who is God, can perfectly know this divine life. It will never be possible for man, not even with the light of heavenly glory, to comprehend the interior of divine life.

As for the will, it will be perfectly satisfied. There will never be an unsatisfied desire.

Wishing and possessing will necessarily go together. "In God, in the sole Good, you shall find everything," says St. Bonaventure. "Do you desire beauty? The just will be as radiant as the sun. Liberty and strength? In heaven the just will be like the angels of God. Vigor? There, health will be eternal. Wisdom and enthusiasm? The blessed will be satisfied with the glory of God, and inebriated with abundance. Harmony? The angels will sing and the heavenly choirs will chant the alleluia. Company and friends? The communion of saints will be found there. Honors and riches? "Wealth and riches shall be in his house..." (Ps. 112:3). Permanence and security? "And his reign will be without end" (Lk. 1:33).

St. Anselm tries to list everything that the souls of the just will possess in heaven: "The hereditary portion of their bliss shall be: beauty, agility, strength, liberty, health, delight, duration, wisdom, friendship, harmony, honor, power, joy, security."

And St. Bernard adds: "Yes, the soul which possesses God cannot desire more; in a single Good, it has found everything that is good."

The bliss of the heart consists in a profound and perfect peace. Dionysius the Areopagite assures us that in this world there is no good so universally coveted, so eagerly sought, so reasonably expected, as peace. Every heart cries out for peace. Even insensible creatures seem to crave peace, and tend toward those perfections which naturally belong to them. This universal appeal for peace is a spontaneous longing for the eternal tranquility that is enjoyed by God and in Him by the blessed.

"Peace!" sang the angels over the stable of Bethlehem to all men of good will.

"Peace!" was the great gift of Jesus, which He left us before ascending to His Father.

"Peace!" was the greeting the first Vicar of Christ gave to the young Church in his first Epistle, and Paul and the other apostles speak of peace, and announce peace.

"Rest in peace!", "In the peace of Christ!" wrote the first Christians on their tombstones.

And the Church, praying for her deceased children, that they be soon admitted to the place of consolation, light, and peace, wishes them heaven. Peace is the synonym for heaven, as light is the synonym of the sun. In the glory of heaven the soul will enjoy perfect peace with God and all His creatures. Perfect peace, because the soul can nevermore lose its Good. If feeling the presence of Jesus in us is sufficient to transform every suffering into joy, what then will be the peace we shall enjoy in heaven, when all trials will be over forever?

"O Jesus," exclaimed the saintly Abbot of Clairvaux, "when You shine on the horizon of a soul, every cloud disappears!"

And since a soul in heaven will be entirely immersed in the divinity of God, heaven is rightly called, "Blessed vision of peace" (from the Liturgy). That is, all the faculties of the soul will be beatified in the vision of God. The intellect will be absorbed by Essential Truth, the will will remain clasped fast to boundless Goodness and become united to it with a changeless love, while the heart will fix itself in divine Beauty.

And God, who all in all is:
"Intellectual light full of love,
Love of true good abounding in gladness,
Gladness that transcends all sweetness"

(Par. c. 20)

will be the eternal joy of all the blessed.

This will be the essential and chief happiness of the blessed, while their secondary and accidental happiness will consist in charity among themselves, in the crown of their personal merits, and in the prerogatives of their glorified bodies after the resurrection.

As to the Body:

The just man will enjoy indescribable delight. His eyes will see the magnificence of heaven; his ears will hear the angelic chorus sing; his olfactory sense will delight in fragrant aromas; his tongue will find joy in blessing God and in conversing with Him.

His body will enjoy attributes similar to those of the glorious body of the Lord Jesus: impassibility, that is, absence of pain, illness, hunger, weariness, or any other discomfort; subtlety — the body will be so spiritual that in its glorified material state it will be able to penetrate solid objects, as the sun's rays penetrate glass; clarity, the power to glow resplendently — like the sun — in the kingdom of the Father; agility, the power to travel unencumbered — the body will acquire a spiritual quality which will give it the power to move swiftly from place to place free from the hindrance of weight or bulk.

"So is it," St. Paul says, "with the resurrection of the dead. What is sown in the earth is subject to decay, what rises is incorruptible. What is sown is ignoble, what rises is glorious. Weakness is sown, strength rises up. A natural body is put down and a spiritual body comes up" (1 Cor. 15:42-44).

In heaven the body will no longer be a hindrance to the perfection of the soul; the struggle between the flesh and the spirit will be ended. The body, most beautiful and luminous, will swiftly go wherever thought determines. The perfection of the body will complement the perfection of the soul, and the two, which on earth were at times irreconcilable enemies, will form in heaven an indissoluble friendship which will last forever.

It is said that an ambassador of Pyrrhus, king of Epirus, who went to Rome when its greatness was at the peak, was impressed with its superb architecture. Astonished by those masterpieces of art, he kept praising the marvels of the Eternal City. His escort, a Roman nobleman, asked him if he had noticed any defect in the city's splendor. "Yes," replied the ambassador, "I noticed a very great defect, and it is that these magnificences must some day end!" But this can never be said of the eternal city of God.

In heaven, says St. Peter, the blessed will possess "an imperishable inheritance, incapable of fading or defilement..." (1 Pt. 1:4).

Will the happiness and glory of the blessed in heaven ever end?

Never.

Can they ever lose heaven?

Nevermore.

Can they ever be separated from God, from His love?

Nevermore.

The words of our Lord Jesus Christ will then come true: "...then your hearts will rejoice with a joy no one can take from you" (Jn. 16:22).

Star From Star...

"Even among the stars, one differs from another in brightness," wrote St. Paul (1 Cor. 15:41).

God is infinitely wise and just; He not only has to establish a place of punishment, hell, for the wicked, and a place of enjoyment, heaven, for the good, but He also has to punish and reward according to the merits of each individual.

Whoever in this life has applied himself to better knowing the Lord by studying the catechism willingly, by listening attentively to sermons and the explanations of the Gospel, in short, by being instructed in religion, will know God better in heaven. Therefore, the more one loves the Lord on earth, the more he will enjoy Him in heaven: this is evident even in our ordinary way of judging things. Is it not just that a St. Francis of Assisi, a St. Francis Xavier, a St. Teresa should enjoy greater glory in heaven than a sinner who has waited till the point of death to convert himself?

Thus, there will be a diversity of vision among the blessed because the difference in merits requires a diverse distribution of reward. Jesus Himself affirms the variation in the happiness of the elect when He says: "In my Father's house there are many dwelling places" (Jn. 14:2).

And St. Paul in his first letter to the Corinthians wrote: "Each will receive his wages in proportion to his toil" (1 Cor. 3:8).

Nevertheless, each of the blessed will possess in himself such a fullness of joy that he cannot wish for more.

Fearing that not everyone in heaven would be completely happy, St. Thérèse of the Child Jesus one day revealed to her sister Pauline her astonishment at the fact that God did not give equal glory to all the blessed in heaven.

"She then sent me to take father's large glass," narrates St. Thérèse in her autobiography, "and placed it near my thimble. Then, filling them both, she asked me to tell which of the two was fuller. I said that I saw them equally full and that it would be impossible to pour into either of them more water than they could hold. Then Pauline made me understand how in heaven the last of the elect would not envy the happiness of the first; and by thus making this most sublime secret understandable to my small mind, she gave my soul the nourishment it needed."

Later on, when Thérèse was a Carmelite sister at Lisieux, she spoke thus of God's justice:

"If to appear before the God of sanctity we must be very pure, from this fact, I know that He is infinitely just, and this justice, which frightens so many souls, forms the theme of my joy and confidence! Justice does not mean only the use of severity against the culprit, but also the acknowledging of good intention and the rewarding of virtue" (*A Story of a Soul*).

Once a devout person asked a priest whether the blessed in heaven envied those who enjoyed a greater degree of blessedness than they.

And the priest answered, "If the blessed could be envious, for that very reason they would no longer be blessed."

Furthermore, there is no discordance of wills in heaven. The will of each elect soul is one with the will of God. Hence, if God varies the degree of happiness of the blessed, the blessed love and wish that variety, and each rejoices over the happiness of the others.

It is true that on earth, when brothers divide an inheritance, they often look at one another with a bit of envy, because each thinks: Too bad your share cannot be mine too!... But in heaven it will not be so; every soul will possess God entirely and will possess Him for all eternity.

Thousands and thousands of centuries will pass (according to our way of speaking), but the blessed will enjoy heaven in the same measure which God allotted to them from the first moment of their entrance into the heavenly fatherland, not even an iota of their happiness being diminished in time.

Could Abraham, Moses, Job, the apostles, the first martyrs of the Christian era, perhaps say: "Now we have already enjoyed a fourth, a tenth, a hundredth of the happiness we are entitled to"?—No, they could not say that. They are always at the very beginning of the enjoyment of their Good.

O heaven, heaven, how beautiful you are! St. Paul prudently counseled us to consider all the goods of this world as mere cast-offs in all our efforts to possess you!

When considering the honors of this world, St. Philip Neri lifted his eyes upward and with good reason exclaimed, "Heaven! Heaven!"

No matter what sacrifices it may cost us to love and serve our Lord, they are worthwhile in view of the great reward that awaits us!

Once, two noblemen, while hunting, found a hermit who lived a very penitent life in a hut in a solitary place. After questioning him about various things, they asked him if he had ever had moments of sadness in his solitude.

"Oh, yes," answered the saintly hermit, "but as soon as I feel sad, I look out that little window and immediately every feeling of sadness disappears and I rejoice."

One of the gentlemen went to look out the window to see if something special could be seen from there. Not finding anything worthy of notice, he asked the hermit what comforted him so much.

"What? Don't you see anything?" asked the hermit.

"Nothing but a bit of sky."

"That's just it," replied the hermit. "It is that bit of heaven which comforts me so greatly."

When we experience sadness or difficulties in the course of our lives; when pain, separation or death come to knock at the door of our hearts; we, too, like that hermit, should lift up our eyes to heaven and repeat with St. Francis of Assisi:

"Of such happiness my hope is bright
That every pain to me is delight."

O heaven, you are a ray of sunshine in the darkness of this world, the only comfort in this valley of tears, the only joy in this exile of sadness!

CHAPTER III

THE GLORIOUS GOAL

Why must I go about in mourning?
(Ps. 43:2)

The Longing of the Exiled....

This could be the title of the tenth chapter of the ninth book of the "Confessions" of St. Augustine, in which, speaking of his mother, the saint wrote: "When the day on which she was to depart from this life was approaching — a day that You knew though we did not — it came about, as I believe by Your secret arrangement, that she and I stood alone leaning in a window, which looked inward to the garden within the house where we were staying at Ostia on the Tiber. There we were away from everybody; we were resting from the weariness of our long journey by land and preparing for the coming voyage by sea. We talked together, she and I alone in deep joy. Forgetting the past and looking forward to the future, we were discussing in the presence of Truth, which You are, what the eternal life of the saints could be like, that which eye has not seen, nor ear heard, nor has entered into the heart of man. Our hearts yearned for the sparkling waters of Your fountain, the fountain of life which is in You. We hoped in some way to grasp the meaning of so great a truth. Our conversation brought us to the conclusion that any bodily pleasure whatsoever, however attractive or delightful, seemed incomparable to the bliss of eternal life and scarcely worthy even of mention. As our love flamed upward toward You, we reviewed, in passing, the various things of earth, up to the heavens themselves, whence sun and moon and stars shine down upon this earth. Soaring ever higher, we contemplated; and speaking together, we marveled at Your works. Finally, we came to consider our own souls, and went beyond to that region of unending joy, where You feed Israel forever with the food of truth. There life is that Wisdom by which all things are made, both the things that have been and the things that are yet to be. But this Wisdom itself is not made. It is as it has ever been, and so it shall be forever. Indeed 'has ever been' and 'shall be forever' have no place in it; it simply '*is*,' for it is eternal, whereas 'have been' and 'shall be' are not eternal. While we were talking thus of Your Wisdom and hungering for it with all our hearts, we attained it for one brief instant. Then, sighing, we reluctantly returned to the sound of our own tongues. The world with all its delights now seemed tawdry in comparison with what we talked of. My mother said, 'Son, for my own part, I no longer find joy in anything in this world. What I am still to do here and why I am here I know not, now that I no longer hope for anything from this world. One hope there was, for which I desired to remain a little longer, that I should see you a Catholic Christian before I should die. This God has granted me most generously, for I now see you His servant, condemning all worldly pleasures. What, then, am I doing here?' What answer I made, I do not clearly remember. Within five days, or not much longer, she fell into a fever; and nine days later she died.''

Thirsting for happiness, our hearts seek it here on earth in vain. The few joys which earthly pleasures procure are false and fleeting.

Our hearts aspire to a happiness that is infinite and lasting; where can it be found?

"You have made us for Yourself, O Lord," St. Augustine says, "and our hearts are restless until they repose in You."

Where can we find happiness? In God.

What About Suffering?

How many times in life do pain, dissatisfaction, and trial tempt us to say, "God has forgotten me! I am unfortunate! If the Lord loved me, He would not permit this or that...." Too often we have forgotten that in this life suffering is inevitable, and that instead of running away from it, we must accept it and evaluate it for its real worth.

Working amid the fumes and din of a factory, the laborer is happy, because he expects his wages.

Traveling through deserted and dangerous regions, in sunshine or in rain, by day or by night, the wayfarer exults in spite of fatigue, because he approaches home and loved ones.

Hiding in trenches or fox holes, between one battle and another, the soldier rejoices in the hope of making his country freer and stronger.

But a hope much greater than any of these, a hope born from suffering, makes the Christian happy — the hope of heaven. For this hope he toils, travels, battles — and sings.

Reevaluate pain, therefore — whether it comes in the form of physical, moral, or spiritual suffering — and change it into precious coin with which to buy heaven. If it is physical suffering, let us reflect that bacteria and pain, while undermining the body, can serve to purify and free the soul. If, instead, it is suffering of the heart and mind, gather with diligence all this suffering as you would precious gold and offer it to the Lord for your sanctification and for the salvation of many others. Particularly, spiritual suffering, which torments our soul, is more than ever a means of purification and ascent into heaven. Let our attitude in the face of suffering be that of complete acceptance and an intelligent evaluation.

Sergius Nicoli, a young Catholic university student of Verona, taught this in a silent sacrifice and with glowing language. In one of his literary works, written on the theme of pain shortly before his death, we read:

"Ah, if only we had a little faith and generous courage, we would bless the Lord for our sufferings, and, despite being troubled by want, perverseness, pain, and violent agitation of misfortune, life would evolve spiritually serene.

"...Elsewhere not here, must we visualize our real fatherland, where we will find recompense for our earthly strife, sweetness of perennial rest, and the exhilaration of a decisive triumph. Here on earth we have only an extended vigil, during which we must, in the faithful service of God, prepare ourselves by toiling for the beautiful Feast of Eternity, until such time as the Lord wills. Be of good heart; when the Feast shall have been served, all the pain, worry and trial we have had to undergo to secure it will seem mere trifles!

"Then, with hands clasped, we shall thank the Lord for having sprinkled our lives with obstacles — not for the sake of the obstacles themselves, nor for the pleasure of seeing us stumble, but because by overcoming them victoriously we change them into so many steps for climbing higher in virtue and merit and, consequently, in heavenly glory."

And elsewhere, using, as he himself called it, a fable that is childish but convincingly logical, he wrote:

"Let us suppose that an inheritance of several million dollars, beautiful palaces, villas, parks and castles, one more magnificent than the other, were available to us upon the sole condition of our receiving a single stroke of a lash well applied.

"Who would be so foolish as to refuse to submit to the ordeal for fear of the momentary pain of a lashing? Why, as soon as it was over, the pain would no longer be felt, and meanwhile, the castles, palaces, villas, parks and millions of dollars would be ours. Well, that imaginary tale gives us an idea of the immense treasure waiting for us at the hands of divine goodness whenever He gives us suffering: paradise eternal, incomparably beautiful, rich, and happy— all this in return for every moment of pain. This being so," concluded the brave youth upon whom life had inflicted much pain, "let pains come by the hundreds, by the thousands! There will be that many more heavens to enjoy forever in the next life."

At times, in the design of divine Providence pain has the further purpose of bringing back to God one who has strayed away or of *preventing* one's straying away.

Francis Coppée wrote in his book, *Knowing How To Suffer:*

"One of my friends, a brilliant poet of a fantastic and dreamy turn of mind, had made up for himself a faith of his own—wholly human in its philosophy. A short time ago he confided to me that his philosophy of human reason had finally met with disaster. 'Yes,' he told me, 'I have spent ten years of my life under the delusion that there is no afterlife, that everything is a dream and a fantasy. My system was working out magnificently and I was happy. But a few weeks ago my little daughter fell ill; the doctor shook his head...and I then joined my wife in kneeling down to pray to the Good God, the heavenly Father, who alone could save her for me in this world and again join us together in the next one.'

"Since then," Coppée continues, "I regard this friend of mine as a new member of the great family of Christ! And others will come...they'll be nudged, directed, pushed, warned by a physical or moral suffering which arrives unexpectedly to tell them: 'I am the messenger of God, who wants you with Him... for your welfare and happiness in the eternal life which awaits you.'"

Ordinarily, we are not courageous enough to ask our Lord to send us sufferings, but let us accept with patience, docility, love and generosity those which we receive from His hands.

St. Thérèse of the Child Jesus so well understood the providential mission of suffering with Christian acceptance that she considered lost the day which passed without any suffering.

Lift up your eyes and fix your gaze upon the heavenly Jerusalem in all its dazzling splendor of glory, sanctity, purity and love. This is our fatherland; walk toward it without allowing yourselvs to be overwhelmed by trials, temptations and suffering.

A famous sculptor once said, "Often, as I square a block of marble and let the chips fly, I pity that mass of marble. And to comfort it I remark, 'I stab you and cut pieces from you, it is true, but I do it to render you eternal by shaping you into a splendid form.'" We know a sculptor far greater even than Phidias; He is our Lord. His marble is man; pain is His chisel.

In suffering, we must say to ourselves, "The Lord taxes my soul because He wants to make it greater and more beautiful."

The sisters in charge of a particular hospital were edified by the fortitude of a certain patient, who suffered greatly but never complained. Medicine, surgery, insomnia, fainting spells always found him calm and smiling; in fact, he was the cheer of the other patients. When the superior inquired about his fortitude, he answered, "Why should I complain and cry? I am the most fortunate man in the world. Day by day disease corrodes the iron chain that keeps me tied to this earth, and within a few months it will grant me the possibility of flying to heaven."

O heaven, desire of suffering humanity, you contain the laurels of all martyrdom, the recompense of all labor, the triumphs of all struggles. To those who are about to weaken in the strife, you show the vast storehouse of your treasures, and then a new hope revives them because of the bright anticipation of possessing you.

On Toward the "Paths of Hope"

Theophane Venard, Martyr of Tonquin, whose name during the past decades has resounded with warm, sympathetic admiration throughout even the remotest regions, said this in a letter that he wrote to his sister, Melanie, from the iron cage in which he was imprisoned:

"In all probability, I will be beheaded; glorious shame, whose reward will be heaven. At this news, dear sister, you will cry, but from happiness. Imagine your own brother crowned with the aureole of the martyrs, the palm of victory in his hand.... A little while yet and my soul shall leave earth and I shall approach my fatherland. I have been victorious and am about to enter the abode of the elect; I am about to see beautiful things which man has never seen, hear harmonies which ears have never heard, enjoy happiness which the human heart has never experienced.

"Although I am still in the arena, I dare to sing the hymn of triumph as if I already had been crowned a victor."

O heaven! You are truly the crown of the battle fought and won of which St. Paul speaks: "I have fought the good fight, I have finished the race, I have kept the faith. From now on a merited crown awaits me; on that Day the Lord, just judge that he is, will award it to me" (2 Tm. 4:7-8).

Heaven is the glorious goal, the earned mantle, the prize, the eternal crown. Then rejoice, O unvanquished defenders of the Faith. Rejoice, holy martyrs of Christ, you of the mutilated bodies, because your torn limbs will be restored to you whole in their glorified beauty and for all eternity.

How many good-byes, how many separations, how many detachments there are in this world! We, too, like the tribes of Israel, should hang our instruments on the weeping willows on the river banks of Babylon, for it is impossible to sing in a land of exile! But when we shall arrive there, in heaven, oh, then what inexpressible happiness! Parents and children will clasp one another again; husbands will open arms to faithful wives; brothers and sisters and friends will meet again and find unending joy in one another's embrace. There the memory of dark hours of anguish and pain endured here below will give increase of bliss.

There will be no mourning and weeping in heaven, because (Sacred Scripture assures us): "He [God] shall wipe every tear from their eyes" (Rv. 21:4).

Having asserted that our country is heaven, St. Cyprian exhorts us:

"Why, then, do we not hurry and run to have a look at our fatherland, to greet our dear ones? A great number of our relatives are waiting for us in heaven. A great and rich multitude of parents, brothers, children, already certain of immortality and solicitous for our salvation, yearns for us.

"O what joy for them and for us, as we enter into their presence and are enfolded in their embraces! What delight in the heavenly kingdom, without the fear of dying and with the joy of living eternally! What supreme and perpetual happiness!... Dearest brothers, with ardent desire, let us make haste to join them and let us yearn to be with them soon."

The hope of a heaven which awaits us sustains, comforts, moderates, and teaches man to work not only for this transitory life, but, above all, for the eternal one, in which he will attain true and everlasting happiness.

The mere thought of the existence of heaven is a most powerful incentive in the battle of good against evil. Nothing but the doctrine of the existence of heaven can give us fortitude in the struggle.

Exhausted is the gentle flower of hope,
Which turns again the weary soul to God.
The best the world can offer to mankind
Is night forlorn and cold oblivion.

Sadly enough, in life the scene that Raphael Sanzio depicted in his famous painting of the Transfiguration seems only too true. At the bottom of the picture is portrayed a child possessed by the devil; its violently contorted limbs, its vivid lips and its eyes, grotesque in convulsion, give it a horrible appearance. In one corner is a kneeling woman, desolation and terror reflected in her countenance. In an open plain depicted nearby stands a group of Jesus' disciples contemplating the ghastly spectacle and sad because of their inability to free the possessed child. A multitude of people, scattered about in various postures of helplessness, stand by without knowing what to do. In the upper portion of the picture we perceive Jesus on Mount Tabor, resplendent with the light of divine beatitude; but below Him, no one thinks of Him; no one asks His help except one lone soul off in a distant corner. With arms outstretched towards Mount Tabor, he seems to be shouting to the others, "There is God! Call on Him for help!" But no one pays heed.

Such is the picture of life, full of sadness and torment, and man is powerless to give consolation and comfort.

Yet above us all there is the eternal Tabor, heaven, where God abides in eternal happiness. Christian hope points to Him. Whereas evils torment and afflict us here below, Christian hope holds out heaven to us. Beholding the vision of the happiness that awaits them, the free, hopeful, serene children of God bravely withstand the miseries of this life.

Once an artillery captain went to visit one of his sisters, a cloistered nun. He was so depressed with the austerity of the convent that he said, "Come away from here, dear sister. Come back to our elegant home, which is furnished with all sorts of comfort.''

The nun shook her head.

The brother persisted, ''But what have you here in your cell that appeals to you?''

''A window.''

''A window? What do you mean? All rooms have windows....''

''And mine even has a broken pane,'' added the sister, ''but it is beautiful....''

''What do you mean?''

''I'll speak more plainly. The window lets me see a bit of sky. Working, reading or praying, I look at the sky thousands and thousands of times a day. At night, from my bed, I can see the stars, the moon...and I think that within twenty—or forty years at the most —I shall soar beyond the clouds and go to heaven.''

Heaven is the goal of our hopes, whether we consider a life spent in the drudgery of menial daily duties or a life like that of St. Paul, heroically lived in continual danger of death.

The shepherd boy who watches his sheep from morning till night will receive the same recompense as the king on whose shoulders weighs the government of a people, ''Because,'' says a certain author, ''the governing of empires or the counting of grains of sand is immaterial to God, as long as both duties are performed according to His divine will.''

We should pass through the vicissitudes of this life with a continuous *sursum corda!* on our lips. Here below, think of heaven and fight the battle of good against evil. Think of heaven as you sing the songs of exile. Think of heaven and perform works worthy of a citizen of heaven and a child of God.

Christian hope holds out heaven to us.
Beholding the vision of the happiness
that awaits them, the free, hopeful,
serene children of God bravely withstand
the miseries of this life.

St. Augustine wrote:

"Here below, let us sing the praises of God, as we think of the day when we shall sing them in heaven. Though here we sing them with trepidation, in heaven we shall sing them with assurance; here as people who must die, there as possessors of eternal life; here in hope, there in reality; here in exile, there in our fatherland.... Let us sing, not to lull ourselves to rest, but to uplift ourselves from hardship. Sing, O brothers, as travelers do—without ceasing. Sing and keep walking forward.

"Onward, ever making progress in good deeds. Make progress in faith and in purity of customs: sing and keep on walking."

Heaven Is Ours

On learning that Jesus was to ascend to the Father, the apostles became pensive and sad. They loved the Master so much—how could they survive after His departure? And He, the Master, how could He have the heart to leave them alone, after they had followed Him faithfully for three years, without His even reconstructing the kingdom of Israel which had been promised them?!

Perceiving their sadness, Jesus said to them: "Do not let your hearts be troubled...I am indeed going to prepare a place for you, and then I shall come back to take you with me, that where I am you also may be" (Jn. 14:1, 3).

Jesus has prepared that place in heaven, not only for the apostles, but for all of us. God created us to occupy the places left vacant by the rebel angels: "he wants all men to be saved," said St. Paul (1 Tm. 2:4). God wants all men to be saved and to go to heaven. Hence, there is a place waiting for us there, a place that is ours by right as Christians; we have been marked on the forehead with the seal of God.

On March 2, 295, in the consulship of Tuscus and Anolinus, a magnificent interchange of words took place between a young draftee, Maximilian, and the proconsul, Dione. The proconsul wanted to impress the insignia of the imperial militia on the young man, but he answered, "I will not receive this worldly sign, and if it is attached to me, I will break it, because it is worthless! I am a Christian; I cannot bear lead on my neck after the seal of my Lord Jesus Christ. Him we Christians serve; Him we follow. He is the Prince of life and the Author of salvation."

Dione forced these alternatives upon him: "Either serve and receive the seal or perish miserably."

Maximilian answered, "I will not perish; my name is already with the Lord."

Oh, yes! Our names are written in heaven!

In fact, Jesus has told us that the just are in His Father's hands and no one can snatch them away from Him (cf. Jn. 10:29). With Him we have acquired a right, "an expectation that is certain of the future glory" (Dante, Par. 25) — the certainty of a hope that permits no confusion.

Here on earth we are accustomed to label with the adjective "mine" all that are really gifts of God; in truth we cannot call ours even the earth that covers our grave — only sins and vices. In heaven, instead, we have something which is ours, absolutely ours, strictly ours: our seat of glory. And because we lost that place through sin, Jesus Christ, with the price of His own Blood, has acquired it again for us. Now it is ours; without our consent no one can take it from us.

St. Paul wrote: "Who will separate us from the love of Christ? Trial, or distress, or persecution, or hunger, or nakedness, or danger, or the sword?... Yet in all this we are more than conquerors because of Him who has loved us. For I am certain that neither death nor life, neither angels nor principalities, neither the present nor the future, nor powers, neither height nor depth nor any other creature, will be able to separate us from the love of God that comes to us in Christ Jesus, our Lord" (Rom. 8:35, 37-39).

No, no creature can separate us from God; no one can make us lose heaven. Only our own wills can do this.

Heaven is ours, but we must want it.

The great Aquinas was asked by his sister, "I want to be a saint; what must I do to become a saint?"

Thomas answered: "If you *want* it, you will be one."

"I want to be the first orator in the Forum and the Senate!" exclaimed Cicero. He studied tirelessly and succeeded; Latin eloquence reached the zenith of its glory.

"I want to create Italian tragedy!" cried Alfieri. He had himself tied to his table, and urging himself on with his "I want, always want, most strongly want," he gave us a work which shines like a star in the firmament of Italian drama.

Yes, heaven is ours, but we must want it.

"I have set before you life and death, the blessing and the curse. Choose life, then..." (Dt. 30:19).

Heaven is for those who at any price choose the way of life, narrow and impeded though it be. It is for those who avoid sin and keep their eyes fixed steadily upon eternal truth, the holy law of God, and the teaching of the Church. It is for those who, in the battle, lift up their souls to hope, because, if the kingdom of heaven can be gained only by exertion, the one who hopes knows how to conquer it with vigor. It is for those who keep in check their tumultuous passions, who resist the unruly desires of their hearts, who flee from occasions of sin. It is for those who lose all to gain the All, who happily overcome every trial, who know how to swim strongly against the current that runs toward damnation. Heaven is for those who think and wish and hope for it constantly. It is for those who suffer and fight, work and pray, forgive and love.

Heaven is for us, people of good will, who seek and want it at any cost.

The Desire for Heaven

Some seek heaven with deeds; others, only with words.

Some labor and spend their days and their energies for heaven; others, instead, do nothing. After the battle of Wittenberg, in which he had fought for nine hours, the Duke of Alba was asked by the King of France whether it was true that, as several witnesses had declared, the sun had stopped for a moment during the battle.

"Sire," the duke answered, "I have had much to do on earth today. I have not had time to look up at heaven."

How many Christians never have time to look up to heaven! Yet, *"homo aeternitatis sum"* — I am a being of eternity. A great preacher used to say, "Look up to heaven and always go forward; remember that we were not born to cast our eyes toward the ground, as animals do, but to hold our heads erect, so as to fix our gaze on our heavenly fatherland."

In one of his brief works, the great Bossuet wrote: "If the sole source of our welfare is here on earth, let us become attached to things of the earth; but if, instead, this visible world can offer us only continuous adversity, if the source of our welfare, the basis of our hope, the sole cause of our salvation is in heaven, let us keep ourselves eternally fired with heavenly desires and aims and breathe nothing but heaven." Up there is our Head. Do we, perhaps, want to sever the Head from the rest of the body? Up there, beyond the clouds, the divine Eagle has soared, and would we, poor eaglets, want to remain here below to wallow in the mire of the earth? Up there is God, most joyous, most blessed; up there, there is also a place for us. He is faithful; on countless occasions He has repeated the promise to reward His faithful servants. Doubt not; He will certainly keep His word: "Let us hold unswervingly to our profession which gives us hope, for he who made the promise deserves our trust" (Heb. 10:23). With confidence in Him who is faithful to His promises, we shall keep our eyes lifted up and keep hope in our hearts; then no one can force us to surrender; for we shall stand upright before the enemy and hold fast in our places. If the enemy of our souls finds us always on our feet and fighting for our eternal reward, he shall not enter. No, he cannot break through.

The hope of going to heaven must be the focal point of all our actions. Even if we were to spend our entire life in continuous mortification and penance, we should not consider ourselves abandoned; on the contrary, we would be most fortunate. The grave is our cradle, and the day of our death is in reality our day of birth. After work, comes rest; after humiliation, glory; after pain, eternal happiness. All this we are taught in that most consoling dogma of the resurrection of the dead.

St. Paul wrote to the Thessalonians: "We would have you be clear about those who sleep in death, brothers; otherwise you might yield to grief, like those who have no hope. For if we believe that Jesus died and rose, God will bring forth with him from the dead those also who have fallen asleep believing in him" (1 Thes. 4:13-14).

Heaven is our heritage! Everything else is destined to disappear. Spring disappears, youth disappears, beautiful colors disappear, years and life disappear. Heaven, on the other hand, is the fatherland of eternal beauty, of eternal spring, of eternal youth.

It was the hope of our forefathers of old, as today it is the holy desire of every Christian—a desire which in St. Paul, the enamored of Christ, became unrestrainable—"I long to be freed from this life and to be with Christ" (Phil. 1:23).

PART III

THE MEANS OF GAINING HEAVEN

O Lord, who shall sojourn in your tent?
Who shall dwell on your holy mountain?
He who walks blamelessly and does justice. (Ps. 15:1-2)

CHAPTER I

LIVING ACCORDING TO GOD

> *"I am the way, and the truth, and the life."*
>
> *(John 14:6)*

There is only one way to reach our ultimate end, heaven: to live as God wants us to live. But what must we do to live according to God? The catechism gives the answer: To live according to God we must, with the help of His *grace,* which is obtained through the *sacraments* and *prayer, believe the truths* revealed by Him and *observe His commandments*—a precise and fundamental answer, sublime and broad in content, a unique and immutable program for men of all generations. And the Church in its sublime mission does nothing else but teach and practice this program, which it unfolds to the entire human race.

We Are Children of the Church

One night a traveler arrived at the edge of a large forest and asked his way of a shepherd who seemed to be familiar with the place. "The way?" asked the shepherd. "Why, it is not easy to find, because there are many paths, and all of them except one lead to a deep canyon that borders the forest. Almost every day many travelers who have not been alerted fall into it. It is out of pity for these that I have taken my place here, at the forest's entrance, so that I may guide them and turn them away from disaster. My children help me, too, and we are all at the disposal of you travelers." The traveler accepted the help which the shepherd offered with such kindness, and they both set off.

The next morning, daybreak found them safe on the other side of the forest. The traveler was then able fully to realize the service the shepherd had given him, for before him gaped the abyss they had avoided.

The shepherd exclaimed, "What a pity to see those who refuse my help for love of independence! They all end at the bottom of the canyon."

This legend beautifully points out the sublime mission which the Church fulfills toward all humanity. Mother and teacher of men, the Church attempts to save us by the truth of her doctrines, by the power of her jurisdiction, and by the grace of her sacraments.

This work of salvation is reflected in the three divisions of the Catholic catechism: *truths to be believed, commandments to be observed, and means of grace.* These three constituents of our religion perfectly satisfy the needs of the human spirit and open the way, narrow but certain, to the kingdom of heaven!

However, like "newborn babies" (1 Pt. 2:2) we must entrust ourselves entirely into the arms of our Mother the Church in a spirit of faith, of obedience, and of love. Thus resting in her motherly arms and nourishing ourselves on the food she prepares for us, we "grow to the full maturity of Christ" (Eph. 4:15), till we assume the perfect likeness of Jesus Christ, "to share the image of his Son" (Rom. 8:29) and thus are made worthy of heaven.

Jesus is the Model whom God the Father offered to all men, so that they might pattern their lives upon a divine example. "I am the way, and the truth, and the life" (Jn. 14:6). No other way leads to heaven, only that of imitating Jesus. He who conforms to the image of the Son of God will be saved; he who does not conform will be damned. Individual holiness will be measured in proportion to conformity with our divine Redeemer.

It is said that one day Charles IX, King of France, asked the famous poet Torquato Tasso who, in his opinion, was the happiest of men?

"God," Tasso promptly answered.

"Everybody knows that," answered the king. "But I'm not asking about God; I am asking about men."

"Then," the poet added, "whoever has made himself more like God than anyone else has."

St. Augustine said that after death the soul will knock at the gate of heaven.

"Who are you?" the voice of Christ will ask from within.

"I was a man," the soul will answer.

And then the same voice will whisper, "How have you treated your body of clay? How have you treated your immortal soul?"

"I am a Christian," the soul will add.

Then Christ will ask, "Let me see your hands; are they wounded like mine? Let me see whether your forehead is crowned with my crown. Where is your baptismal robe? Where is the lighted lamp of your faith? Show me your face, so that I may recognize you as my brother...as the son of my Father... as the temple of the Spirit of Love...."

Christian life, allowed full development, assures us of heaven. Christian life is really a preparation for heavenly life. Reason confirms this truth. As a matter of fact, preparation for something means doing those things that are necessary to reach the end that is intended. The end for which man strives is supreme happiness, the perfect knowledge and love of God.

Therefore, preparation for the next life consists in an all-out effort directed to knowing and loving God.

Such is the end for which God has created us: *To know, to love, and to serve Him in this life, and to enjoy Him in heaven.*

This implies a threefold duty for every Christian:

To know God by our intelligence in the study of His perfection and His works, by diligently learning all the truths which the Church proposes for our belief through homilies and religious instruction, and by being on the alert so as to flee from anything — such as bad company, bad literature, etc. — which might cause us the loss of faith.

To love God by proving ourselves to be truly His children, by giving Him the place He deserves in our heart — the first place — and by excluding all worldly affection which He condemns.

Finally, *to serve Him* by doing good, by observing God's holy laws and the laws of the Church, and by fulfilling the obligations of our state and position in life.

CHAPTER II

TRUTHS TO BE BELIEVED

> *"I am the truth."*
> *(Jn. 14:6)*

What must a Christian believe to save his soul?

Only a few things, but he must believe to the point of being willing to shed his blood for them.

An episode which took place during the First World War was related to us thus by a soldier: "On August 20, 1915, we were at Morhange, in Alsace. In the afternoon, we started an attack; enemy projectiles soon whistled frightfully in the air about us. One of my comrades fell at my side, seriously wounded. He kept asking for a priest...but there was none nearby. He felt his life ebbing away fast.

"With a supreme effort, the dying man then raised himself a little, dipped a finger in his wound, and with his own blood, wrote on the ground: *'I believe in God.'*"

Only a few truths are necessary for our belief: the very same truths we learned from the catechism when we were little children in religion class—the very same truths repeated and elaborated upon Sunday after Sunday in the sermons our pastor preached for our spiritual growth during the Mass. But we must be masters of these few truths; we must let them seep into our veins drop by drop, even at the expense of sorrow or sacrifice, so that, if need be, we, too, may write in our own life-blood the truth: "I believe in God."

113

8. Heaven

What are these few truths? They are found in the Apostles' Creed, the commandments of God and of the Church, the sacraments, the Our Father — briefly, the little *catechism* whose pages can render us more learned than that philosopher we mentioned some pages back, who believed that he had seen the answer to all questions about life and that he had fathomed the mysteries of this world, yet destroyed himself uttering the futile query, "Oh, what use is life?" Any number of even the most simple people, including children, could have answered that question for him: "To serve and glorify God, and one day to merit heaven." Indeed, in these simple words from the catechism can be found more vital truth than in the hundreds upon hundreds of pages written by that unfortunate ninety-year-old philosopher.

The Church helps us to live the Christian religion by breaking into small bits the bread of truths that we must digest, truths that are summed up in the Apostles' Creed, in the first pages of the catechism. Our intelligence is shaped at the school of the divine Master, "who enlightens every man who comes into the world" (cf. Jn. 1:7).

By studying divine truths, we learn how much God has bestowed upon man — as Creator, in the natural order; as Redeemer and Sanctifier, in the order of grace; and as Supreme Judge, in the afterlife. In a word, we learn all the truths concerning our eternal salvation as they have been preached by our divine Savior and His apostles, and as they are promulgated by the Church to all the faithful until the end of time.

Many fundamental truths can be known through human reason; these include the existence of God, the immortality of the soul, and all the moral truths contained in the Decalogue.

There are other truths, however, which we would never know if God had not revealed them to us. These are: the distinction in God between nature and person; the existence of the angels; the possibility, through grace, of reconciling and elevating ourselves to a union with God. By virtue of revelation, this second order of truths is reasonably clear to human intelligence.

Finally, there is a third order of truths, which, both before and after revelation, absolutely transcend the capacity of human reason. Even the man who possesses the most profound intelligence can never succeed in explaining them only in the light of reason. These are the so-called mysteries.

Now, which and how many of these truths must a Christian believe in order to have enough faith to be saved?

Of course, religious instruction can be more or less adequate, according to the mental capacity and training of the faithful. For instance, the religious instruction that a child is able to absorb is one thing; what an adult is obliged to receive is another. Again, the instruction that an intellectual can acquire is one thing; that which an unlettered person can absorb is another.

But there is a minimum of religious instruction which is necessary for all in order to be saved, and this is a sufficient knowledge of the two principal mysteries of our holy Faith: the unity and trinity of God and the incarnation, passion, and death of our Lord Jesus Christ. In other words, we must acquire a sufficient knowledge of God Himself, of the incarnation of the Son of God and of the redemption. Besides all this, we must acquire a sufficient knowledge of the Church, of the sacraments, of the duties imposed

on us by the Decalogue, and, finally, of what awaits
us after death. To believe these truths, whether they
are comprehensible or incomprehensible to our reason,
is a definite obligation for every Christian. In other
words, we can say that there is a single Creed for both
the unlearned children of Adam as well as for the
learned and the wise. It is one sole Creed, drawn up,
as are the answers of the catechism, in a brief, concise
and harmoniously coordinated formula containing
the truths taught by Jesus Christ to the apostles, and
through them to all the nations of the earth. These
are the very same truths which the world has been
listening to for nineteen centuries, always the same,
whereas the doctrines devised by men, changing constantly, are even in contradiction with and destructive
of one another.

> I believe in God, the Father Almighty,
> Creator of heaven and earth. I believe in
> Jesus Christ, His only Son, our Lord.
> He was conceived by the power of the
> Holy Spirit and born of the Virgin Mary.
> He suffered under Pontius Pilate, was
> crucified, died, and was buried. He de-
> scended to the dead. On the third day He
> rose again. He ascended into heaven, and
> is seated at the right hand of the Father.
> He will come again to judge the living
> and the dead. I believe in the Holy Spirit,
> the holy catholic Church, the communion
> of saints, the forgiveness of sins, the
> resurrection of the body, and life ever-
> lasting.

These are the truths which the Fathers and Doc-
tors of the Church have explained and eloquently

interpreted in their profound writings and for which millions of martyrs gave their lives. These are the same truths which the Pope teaches from Vatican hill, and the missioner repeats in the lowliest, most primitive hut. These are the unchanging truths which resound from the lips of most eminent preachers beneath the sweeping vaults of the most magnificent cathedrals, or loving mothers repeat tenderly to the cherished offspring at their knees. They are always the same truths, immutable and eternal; no one may even dare add or take away from the word of God.

These truths are the very ones which the catechism proffers for our belief, invites us to hope with, and prescribes as a code of life. The catechism, the book of life, contains the science of God and of men, of the angels and of the world; and it is the only book that does not leave unanswered any of the great questions which affect humanity.

The testimony left us by the philosopher Juffroy, an unbeliever and a rationalist, is remarkable in this regard: "There is a little book which is taught to little children...the catechism. Read this little book, and in it you will find the solutions to all the questions I have placed before your consideration. Ask a Christian where the human race comes from; he knows it. Ask that little child, who does not as yet know life, why he is here in this world and what he will be after death; he will give you a sublime answer, which, perhaps, he does not understand but which is nonetheless admirable. Ask him how the world was created and to what end, why God has placed animals and plants in it, how the earth was peopled, why men speak many languages, why they suffer, why they struggle—he knows. The origin of the world, the origin of the human species, questions of race, man's destiny in this and in the next life, the relations of man with God, the duties of man towards his fellowman, the rights of man over creation — nothing is unknown to him!"

All this is in the catechism, in that humble little book to which the learned are constrained to resort after they have asked in vain of philosophy the solution to the great problems of life.

How beautiful is faith, how holy is religion!

There are moments in which the most exalted and most incomprehensible truths appear so clear to our minds as to make us feel that, truly, religion is like the sun, which illuminates all things. Then, enraptured by invisible wonder, we feel moved to preach to the whole world the sacred truths of faith in compliance with the divine mandate: "Go and teach all nations."

In a moment when the torch of his faith gave off a livelier spark, unbeliever Victor Hugo once said: "That which lightens our burdens, sanctifies work, and makes man strong, wise, patient, kind and meanwhile humble, great, worthy of the gift of intelligence, worthy of liberty, is this: having before one's eyes the perpetual vision of a better world, which shines through the shadows of this life."

Unfortunate indeed is he who has never tasted the sweetness of faith; believing is so great a joy and consolation that in comparison with it all the pleasures of this world become nothing but bitter, revolting passions.

CHAPTER III

OBSERVANCE OF THE COMMANDMENTS

"I am the way."
(Jn. 14:6)

The Freedom of the Children of God

In a lengthy discourse that He gave to the Jews, Jesus spoke about His divine mission and said to those who believed in Him: "If you live according to my teaching, you are truly my disciples; then you will know the truth, and the truth will set you free" (Jn. 8:31-32). Here is solemnly proclaimed the freedom that belongs to the children of God—that freedom which is a humble, complete and absolute subjection of our minds to the truth. It is the "reasonable homage" of which St. Paul spoke.

Now, the study of the catechism leads us to a supreme liberation of spirit, which, more than the hope of the mind, is the aspiration of the heart and the enlargement of all life. A soul set free through the study of the truths of our holy religion can say: I do not depend on any creature. I have with me all that I need! I am self-sufficient. Coming from creatures, this may seem loathsome pride. Instead, it is a sincere affirmation of real joy.

What more, indeed, could a person need, when all is provided by God, his loving Father, whom he, by loving, possesses within himself? Who among men could better provide for his countless needs or satisfy the yearnings of his heart, the hopes of his soul? The soul can justly say: Except for God, I have need of nothing and, furthermore, nothing else would satisfy me. The good things of this world do not appeal to me, nor do passing evils frighten me.

My God, who is in me, is my all.

But only in the truth of Christian doctrine, which has given us true freedom, can such declarations be made without falling into monstrous error. Only he who remains upon the heights can say that he possesses true and perfect liberty of spirit. He who descends from that level becomes a menial, necessarily a menial, because he places himself at the mercy of creatures and creature comforts.

Lift up your hearts to God! To God, who is our Creator and our Redeemer, our life, our happiness, and our glory in heaven.

We were created to love Him, we were redeemed to love Him again after the fall, and He wants nothing else from us but love, an intelligent and active love, according to the exhortation of St. Paul: "Let us profess the truth in love" (Eph. 4:15). This love leads us to the sincere observance of the commandments of God and of the Church and of the duties of our state. Thus we shall recognize in creatures the image of the Creator, so that we shall love them in Him and for Him. Finally, ours shall be a love which, as Jesus taught us, sums up the whole law.

Many are the aids and attractions that make the practice of this love easy! Among them are these: the sacraments; Holy Mass; the intercession of the Blessed Virgin, our Mother; the brotherly ministry of the angels and of the saints, our advocates. Then, to spur us to a wholesome fear, there are thoughts of approaching death and judgment, of the horrors of hell, of the indescribable delights of heaven. Finally, there is the spectacle of Jesus crucified, a God hung on the cross for love of us. All these are ours to enjoy or to contemplate.

An entire supernatural world opens before the Christian who, instructed in these truths, lives an active faith which yields the fruits of eternal life. In practice he does not separate dogma from morality! St. James' declaration that faith without works is dead is extremely clear to him. By this time, he has rendered himself worthy of the incomparable gift of true freedom, and he lives it in the spirit of the children of God. Truth has made him free.

Good Works for Eternal Life

After the first essential duty of our holy religion, belief in God, comes that of obedience to God. While the first subordinates our intelligence to God through faith, the second subordinates our will in practical life.

Our first duty involves the truths to be believed about God; the second involves keeping the Commandments of God.

Truly, in order to be saved it is not enough to be baptized and believe the truths that the Church teaches; it is also necessary to obey God by observing His Commandments.

A young man asked Jesus:

"Teacher, what good must I do to possess everlasting life?" (Mt. 20:16) And Jesus answered him: "If you wish to enter into life, keep the commandments."

"Which ones?" (Mt. 20:17-18)

And Jesus listed them: "'You shall not kill'; 'You shall not commit adultery'; 'You shall not steal';

'You shall not bear false witness'; 'Honor your father and your mother'; and 'Love your neighbor as yourself'" (Mt. 20:18-19). Thus, in a few words, all the ancient law was summed up!

On another occasion Jesus warned: "None of those who cry out, 'Lord, Lord,' will enter the kingdom of God but only the one who does the will of my Father..." (Mt. 7:21) — that is, he who keeps the Commandments.

The observance of the Commandments, always possible with the help of grace, is absolutely necessary for salvation. It is true that this observance may prove burdensome in particular instances; but we must not forget that the present life is a life of trial, and as such it naturally requires renunciation and sacrifice, which are destined, however, to merit for us perfect and eternal happiness as the reward for our fidelity on earth.

The ten Commandments resemble the twelve articles of faith because of their concise style; they are brief statements, terse and to the point, ample in significance, and far-reaching in scope. They are applicable to all the circumstances of life and human activity, personal or social, private or public, interior or exterior.

1. I, the Lord, am your God. You shall not have other gods before me.
2. You shall not take the name of the Lord, your God, in vain.
3. Remember to keep holy the Lord's day.
4. Honor your father and your mother.
5. You shall not kill.
6. You shall not commit adultery.
7. You shall not steal.

8. You shall not bear false witness against your neighbor.

9. You shall not covet your neighbor's wife.

10. You shall not covet anything that belongs to your neighbor.

The observance of the Commandments leads to life that is Christian in its entirety, while it obtains the choicest blessings from heaven. We read in the Sacred Scriptures that our Lord used to promise even temporal blessings to those who observed the Commandments: "But if you obey the voice of Yahweh your God faithfully, keeping and observing all those commandments of his that I enjoin on you today... all the blessings that follow shall come up with you and overtake you.... You will be blessed in the town and blessed in the country. Blessed will be the fruit of your body, the produce of your soil, the issue of your livestock, the increase of your cattle, the young of your flock. Blessed will be your pannier and your bread bin. Blessed will you be coming in, and blessed going out.... Yahweh will summon a blessing for you...in all your undertakings..." (Dt. 28:1, 2, 3-6, 8) (JB).

God's ways do not change, nor does the system or the economy of His government. This generous promise of blessings upon the ancient Hebrews who observed the Law is also attested to in our day by those who faithfully observe the Commandments of God.

The sociologist La Play, who in his economic surveys had the opportunity of questioning more than ten thousand European families, came to a conclusion very far from what had originally been expected, but nonetheless precious and consoling. He ascertained and left on record that "The families in which he had found peace and a greater degree of well-being were those in which the holy Commandments of God were observed."

What more encouragement do we need "to run with an open heart," as the Psalmist says, in the way of the Commandments?

The holy Curé of Ars used to say to his parishioners, "Oh, how beautiful to do everything with God! You will work while He will bless your labor; you will walk while He will bless your steps; you will struggle, you will suffer with Him...." How consoling it is to think that God always sees us in all our actions! Let us then say every morning, "Today I will live in such a way as to please the Lord."

And all shall be taken note of: the renunciation of a look, of a motion, of a little satisfaction, all shall be written down.

And the saint concludes, "For a soul that has faith, the thought of living with God as with bosom friends is truly consoling, for with such a friend hours go by like minutes and one enjoys a foretaste of heaven."

Therefore, a life which foreshadows the joys of heaven, full of the blessings of heaven and of earth, is reserved for those who in humility of spirit and fervor of faith observe the holy Commandments of God, and live totally that Christian life which is — to quote the majestic words of Pope Pius XII — "to suffer hardships as Christians."

Christian Life

Christian life means living according to the teachings of the Gospel, according to the way of Jesus, according to the way of grace and the sacraments.

Pope Pius XII presented an admirable picture of what the great family of Christianity must be when the fluid of Christian life circulates in all its members.

"Up there, higher up, is our permanent fatherland. We were born for it, to it we are destined to go and toward it we are directed; and we are journeying with all our brothers in faith and hope, joined by that charity which is greater than faith and hope...charity which attracts and carries along with it all brethren to make them eternal companions in heaven in the blessed sight of God." Here is, in its entirety, Christian life, with the indispensable addition of the apostolate, which is cooperation with the work of our Lord Jesus in the redemption and salvation of souls.

What magnificent serenity is represented here, and in a different degree the same holy serenity is to be found in the peace of any domestic hearth presided over by Christ, ruled by His law and blessed by His cross.

"A real heaven on earth," Pope Pius XI called that home in which harmony reigns with reciprocal love and respect among its members, and which is permeated by an atmosphere of piety and purity. Such a home resembles that of the holy family of Nazareth, from which it draws its inspiration. Such a home can then call itself a true domestic sanctuary, a wholesome retreat of the parish and of society.

Over the past years, several congresses dealing with parish life have been convened. The purpose of such congresses is to bring parish life back to its former intimate warmth. Parish life means Christian life in its essentially genuine characteristic. Nowadays Christian life also means living an organized life of apostolate. It is the duty of every Christian to enroll himself as a member in apostolic parish associations. Apostolate is an essential part of Christian life. Furthermore, the members of such associations receive the best religious and civil training, preparing them for a serene life in the conscientious fulfillment of the duties of their own positions in life. This is the express desire of the Holy Father; and this, for a Christian, should be reason enough to want to be in the vanguard of the glorious army which, under the banner of Christ the King, works for the coming of His kingdom on earth.

Of course, it is obvious that parents as well as their children will find in apostolic societies that moral, intellectual and religious aid which is indispensable in fulfilling life's real mission. How beautiful it is to observe those families whose members are enrolled in the various apostolic societies. In such families, it is easy to live a fully Christian life, whose fruits inevitably bring peace and reciprocal love in this life and secure hope of heaven in the next.

What Bars Heaven?

In this world there is a disastrous reality that bars the gates of heaven, that often prevents the lifting of our eyes to heaven, that razes to the ground the magnificent work of the Redemption: it is mortal sin. Mortal sin, inflicting death upon the soul, prevents it from participating in the merits of Jesus Christ. Thus, it causes one to lose his right to heaven. Oh, if we could understand what it means to lose the right to the heritage of heaven!

Sin causes us to lose heaven and merit hell.

The world may laugh at the mention of sin, because it does not know what a heinous crime it is, but

"Up there, higher up,
is our permanent fatherland.
We were born for it,
to it we are destined to go
and toward it we are directed...."

—Pope Pius XII

faith shows us its effects: the death of the Son of God, the spiritual death of mankind, the inextinguishable fire of hell.

And what about the soul? Unfortunately, the sad effects of sin in the soul are not seen externally; often a body full of life and beauty houses a soul which is dead and horribly disfigured.

What if death should unexpectedly strike a soul in such a state?

A nobel lady traveling on a cable car at Semmering, near Vienna, anxiously asked the conductor — when the train suspended between heaven and earth had nearly reached the summit — what would happen if the cable should break.

"We would apply the brakes," the conductor answered.

"And if the brakes should not hold?"

"We would apply the double safety brakes."

"And if they, too, would not work?"

"Then," the conductor told her, "we would all go either to heaven or hell, each according to his own merits."

The conductor was right. The state of the soul at the moment of death will determine the happy or unhappy destiny which the soul will meet; and that is why Holy Scripture warns us: "Whether a tree falls to the south or to the north, wherever it falls, there shall it lie" (Eccl. 11:3).

We can foresee on what side the tree will fall. Pedrini once wrote, "When a tall tree is rooted out, the woodmen, before cutting the last root, step back to see on which side the top of the tree leans, because the tree will fall precisely on that side." Hence, we too, can guess even now how we shall die. If we lean toward the side of great love of God, we shall die happy; if toward that of sin, the opposite will take place.

While here on earth, we must constantly consider our supernatural destiny. We must regard the earth as a place of transit or exile and not as a definite and permanent abode—as a place of trial and strife and not as a place of inaction and rest.

We must lean towards heaven as the only end worthy of our desires and our efforts, as the only good which can fully satisfy our desire for happiness, as our only real fatherland.

Lean towards God with all your hearts, with all your being. Be ready to sacrifice everything rather than displease Him and run the risk of losing your soul.

Speaking of heaven to his people of Hippo, St. Augustine once said, "Let us suppose that God promised that you should live one hundred, even one thousand years, in the abundance of every good thing of the earth, but on condition that you should not live with Him thereafter...." A mighty cry went up from the whole assembly: "Let everything perish, but let God remain with us!" And so it is. "What profit would a man show if he were to gain the whole world and destroy himself in the process? What can a man offer in exchange for his very self?" (Mt. 16:26)

9. Heaven

CHAPTER IV

PRAYER

"I am the life."
(John 14:6)

Man's life in this world may be compared to a steam locomotive, which needs steel rails to run on. Rails, however, are not sufficient; steam, too, is needed. It is absolutely necessary that a fire be kept going in the boiler, and that it reach the intensity of heat to produce a pressure of steam sufficient to activate the pistons in the engine, and thus set the locomotive in motion. The same may be said of Christian life. Faith guides the mind, as law guides the will. But these guides are not enough if the heart is not animated by a fire which helps to motivate man on the road of virtue toward heaven. This fire is the holy love of God, kept alive through prayer.

Before speaking of the necessity of prayer, however, it is appropriate to give priority to a few words on the value of grace, which is the beginning of Christian life, and about the duty of increasing it by faithful cooperation on our part.

The Power of Grace

If only we could see, as we clearly shall in heaven, what a store of glory a soul can accumulate on earth by faithful correspondence to grace, we would be far more concerned about obtaining an abundance of sanctifying grace for ourselves.

The word "grace" has various meanings. In itself, it implies beauty, harmony and proportion. Sometimes it also signifies favor or blessing; but the theological meaning of sanctifying grace is, according to the definition in the catechism: *"that supernatural gift inhering in our souls and, therefore, habitual which makes us saints; that is, friends and adopted children of God, brothers of Jesus Christ, and heirs of heaven.*

Grace "inheres in" our souls and, therefore, is purely *gratuitous*. It comes from the infinite love God has for us. It is a *supernatural* gift surpassing all nature, and, inasmuch as we could never merit it by ourselves, a gift that God grants solely so that we may attain eternal life in heaven.

Grace is a gift "inhering in our souls and, therefore, habitual." By *"inherent"* we mean to say that it is not a property of the soul, but an added perfection, which intrinsically elevates it to the point of its becoming a sharer of the divine nature: "...sharers of the divine nature" (2 Pt. 1:4). Furthermore, grace makes us saints; that is, "friends, and adopted children of God, brothers of Jesus Christ, and heirs of heaven."

First of all, sanctifying grace removes sin—both original and actual—from the soul, then confers upon it justice and holiness, by which man again becomes innocent, just and holy—as he was when he came forth from the creative hand of God. Sanctifying grace makes the soul capable of knowing God, of loving Him, of possessing Him, and of dwelling with the angels and saints for all eternity.

The real miracle that grace accomplishes is that of conferring on man the infinite dignity of a child of God. A child of God! Yes, sanctifying grace elevates us to this sublime dignity, in comparison to which the most exalted dignities of this world are as nothing. It is said of Leonidas, Origen's father, that he was accustomed to rise during the night and, carefully uncovering the breast of his son, kiss it reverently, because, he said, it was the temple of the Holy Spirit.

The Catholic Duke of Corinthia was surrounded by barons and vassals who were not Christians. Since these showed that they considered human dignity of greatest importance, while they spurned all religious values, the duke one day decided to give an edifying lesson. He invited these men to a magnificent feast, to which he also invited some of his subjects who were poor but faithful Christians. In a magnificent hall, he had a rich and gorgeous table prepared, at which he seated his Christian subjects, whom he had served with dishes of gold and crystal, set by elegantly dressed pages. In the same hall, he seated the barons and the vassals at an ordinary table and had them served with ordinary dishes and silverware. The barons and vassals tried hard to maintain a respectful behavior toward the duke; nevertheless, they let it be seen that they were offended by this treatment.

Then the duke smiled kindly and told them, "Please don't be offended by this unequal treatment. You are dear to me, you are my barons, vassals, and friends; but I must honor these others more because, being Christians, they are the friends and the children of God Himself. They possess a supernatural dignity and merit the utmost respect."

The lesson was effective. Many of the nobles proceeded to study Christianity, and soon became converts.

The real difference among men is determined by grace. Either they possess grace, and are children of God destined to live with Him eternally, or they do not possess grace and are only walking corpses destined to eternal death. All else is of minor importance.

What about beauty—what is its real value? One may well write down zero. What about riches?—Zero. What about high social position, culture, genius, or power?—Zero. Is the grace of God present? Now you may write the digit 1 before all the zeros: Grace is the only single factor that can give those zeros real value.

With a most virile tongue, St. Paul makes us understand this truth: "If I have all the eloquence of men or of angels, but speak without love, I am simply a gong booming or a cymbal clashing. If I have the gift of prophecy, understanding all the mysteries there are, and knowing everything, and if I have faith in all its fullness, to move mountains, but without love, then I am nothing at all. If I give away all that I possess, piece by piece, and if I even let them take my body to burn it, but am without love, it will do me no good whatever" (1 Cor. 13:1-3) (JB).

Here charity is the synonym of grace; hence, with grace, we have everything; without grace, we have nothing.

Yet, how many are they who never think of grace? How many really know and esteem it? How many try to acquire it, sustain it, and increase it? Oh, how saddening is the behavior of those who, for hollow, passing pleasure, lose this priceless gift of God!

Grace is first acquired in Baptism, and it is increased by prayer and good works. It is lost by mortal sin but can be regained by repentance—by obtaining pardon through the Sacrament of Penance or through perfect contrition accompanied by the intention of going to confession.

The Channels of Grace

In what way does the vital stream of grace pass from the adored Head of the Mystical Body, Jesus Christ, to us, His members?

What are the transmitting channels?

Here they are: each sacrament is a transmitting channel of grace. In every sacrament Christ confers a special grace to all who receive that sacrament without setting up spiritual barriers.

First of all, we have the sacrament of *Baptism*, which is the door or gateway to all the other sacraments. By creating in us *the new man*, living the life of Jesus, Baptism causes us to be born to a life of grace. In this sacrament, we draw up a contract with God; that is, we solemnly pledge ourselves (in the baptismal promises) to renounce the devil, his works and his allurements, and to abide solely by the doctrines and laws of Jesus Christ.

Baptism gives us the right to enter that blessed eternity which, in due time, we shall reach if we remain faithful to the sacred promises made. Fidelity to our baptismal promises keeps the gate of heaven open to us.

By the sacrament of *Confirmation*, we are more perfectly bound to the Church, into which we were first incorporated at Baptism. In this sacrament the Holy Spirit gives us an increase of grace, faith, hope, love and the seven gifts that make us sensitive to God's inspirations. He strengthens us to profess and defend the Faith by word and example, as true witnesses of Christ. (We witness to Christ by knowing and loving our Faith, by living it in all respects, by defending it, and by sharing it with others.)

Furthermore, to make up for the losses suffered in the daily struggle to maintain our spiritual state,

God has supplied us with the heavenly Bread of the *Eucharist*—divine food for our souls. In the sacrament of the Eucharist, we receive not only an increase of grace but also the very Author of grace. Jesus becomes the food of our souls and, little by little, transforms us into Himself by transmitting to us His spirit, His sentiments, His virtues, and above all, His love for the Eternal Father and for mankind.

The necessity of going to Holy Communion in order to have eternal life is clear from the words of Jesus: "I myself am the living bread come down from heaven. If anyone eats this bread he shall live forever..." (Jn. 6:51). And He continues: "Let me solemnly assure you, if you do not eat the flesh of the Son of Man and drink his blood, you have no life in you. He who feeds on my flesh and drinks my blood has life eternal and I will raise him up on the last day" (Jn. 6:53-54).

If afterwards we should fall into mortal sin, which extinguishes the life of grace in us, then the sacrament of *Penance,* washing away all our faults in the Blood of Jesus, restores us to the state of innocence, and the golden gates of heaven reopen before us.

When death comes knocking at our door and stirs up a terrible storm of fear, anguish and agony, it is the sacrament of the *Anointing of the Sick,* which, with the holy oil, fills us with the grace of relief and spiritual consolation and animates our hope with those same sentiments with which St. Paul was stirred on the eve of his death: "I have fought the good fight... from now on a merited crown awaits me..." (2 Tm. 4:7, 8). Then man's soul shall rejoice, as the Psalmist says, because of what it has been told: "I rejoiced because they said to me, 'We will go up to the house of the Lord'" (Ps. 122:1).

These five sacraments we have mentioned are ordained to sanctify man in his individual life, while the other two, *Holy Orders* and *Matrimony*, contribute to the building up of the entire Mystical Body. Therefore, for man at any age, for every circumstance in life, for every individual and social duty, there is the grace of the sacraments which, while making the fulfillment of his duties easier, admirably increases in him that treasury of glory which one day he will enjoy in the blessedness of eternity.

Increase of grace brings about a corresponding increase of glory; the sacraments give us all this if we receive them with the proper dispositions. One of the dispositions which enable a person to receive the sacraments well is an intense desire for them. Another is fervent, reverent reception. An intense desire to receive the sacraments is a sign that the soul is hungry and thirsty for holiness. Upon such a soul is invoked Jesus' word, "Blessed!" for that soul shall then be satisfied. Fervor makes the soul warm and establishes within it a happy disposition to refuse nothing to God and to cooperate with Him in the work of self-sanctification.

Cooperation with Grace

The time has passed when it was believed that only contemplative souls were able to attain spiritual heights.

"Holiness," said Pope Benedict XV, "consists in doing the will of God moment by moment."

If we could penetrate into the inmost depths of souls, we would see how God's grace works more profoundly where it finds greater simplicity, greater humility, greater spirit of sacrifice, and greater denial of all that the world holds in esteem. If we could only delve closely into certain aspects of the lives of simple, common people, of mothers of families, of the humble poor, and consider every painful circumstance of their existence, we would pass from wonder to wonder in learning about the heroic sanctity created by grace in faithful souls.

One day, the celebrated Michelangelo was asked by one of his admirers, "How are you able to create with your chisel masterpieces so magnificent that they remain immortal?" Michelangelo answered, "It is all there in the marble; one has only to know how to draw it out."

Oh, yes, it is all in the marble! We need only to take in hand our own chisel and hammer away without self-pity; let the chips of our defects and of our imperfections fly off. Then, little by little, our rough block of marble will show the first outlines of a beautiful statue, which, by patient and constant work, sustained by the grace of God, will gradually evolve into perfection.

How comforting is the thought that all that we do — be it even a desire, a word, a single little sacrifice — may be fixed in a blessed eternity to be our crown of glory. "The fact is that whether you eat or drink — whatever you do — you should do all for the glory of God" (1 Cor. 10:31). What counts is love. In our material preoccupations, we must accumulate wealth for eternal life. Certain souls reach the point of tasting the delight of heaven in their daily lives; these are the souls which nurture themselves with the Eucharist. Since, in a certain sense, the Eucharist contains heaven, these souls with their lively faith and ardent love, may catch an advance glimpse of heaven through the Eucharistic veil.

Grace works marvels, but exacts loving cooperation from us.

A gentleman converted by St. Vincent de Paul, who had well understood what a treasure it is to be a Christian, a son of God, embraced a sincerely Christian life and desired not only to sustain but also to increase divine grace. After having renounced all that he had loved and pursued in life, he one day asked himself, "What more can I offer to God in appreciation for the marvelous grace of having made me a Christian? How else can I show Him all my love and fidelity?" While he was thus musing, his gaze fell upon the sword hanging at his side. He had always carried it honorably. As he recalled the proud glory it had brought him, his whole frame recoiled in an anguish of regretful anticipation of parting with it. But without hesitation he drew the sword from its scabbard and heroically broke it, as he declared, "It shall never be said that I kept anything that prevented me from being completely Yours!"

What an admirable example of cooperation with grace!

The epistle which the Church reads to us in the first Mass of Christmas is a miniature treatise of dogmatic, moral and ascetical theology, and contains a program of life for the Christian:

"The grace of God has appeared, offering salvation to all men. It trains us to reject godless ways and worldly desires, and live temperately, justly, and devoutly in this age as we await our blessed hope, the appearing of the glory of the great God and of our Savior Christ Jesus. It was he who sacrificed himself for us, to redeem us from all unrighteousness and to cleanse for himself a people of his own, eager to do what is right" (Ti. 2:11-14).

Through his disciple Titus, St. Paul exhorted the faithful to cooperate with grace and suggested to them a way of life which, as it kept them away from sin, isolated them from earth and prepared them for heaven.

To cooperate with grace means to live a Christian life in all its fullness; it means to flee, as from a plague, sin in all its forms, and to do good wholeheartedly — to follow faithfully in the footsteps of the Divine Master from Bethlehem to Calvary. It means to be in love with the divine Eucharist and to practice, with simplicity and fervor, devotion to the Virgin Mother of God. It means to develop within ourselves a profound humility, which will make us feel all our unworthiness and weakness and will stimulate us to pray with unlimited confidence and perseverance. Humility and confidence in God are the railroad tracks on which free will travels with the assurance of arriving at its heavenly destination. At the cost of whatever sacrifice, it means the faithful fulfillment of the duties of our positions in life and the acceptance with unwavering love of both the successes and the adversities of life from the hand of God. It means, above all, following the advice of the Divine Master: "Be on guard and pray..." (Mk. 14:38), and keeping it ever in mind that grace flees from sin as light repels darkness and life repels death.

Together with St. Ignatius of Loyola, let us acquire the habit of asking the Lord for this inestimable gift: "Give me only Your love and Your grace, Lord, and I am rich enough. I ask for nothing else."

If we do not resist God's grace, if we place no obstacles in its path, if we let ourselves be infused with its saving current, then we shall witness a renewal of the miracle of an unbelieving and persecuting Saul changed into an apostle and a vessel of election; the miracle of a public sinner changed into a renowned penitent and a great saint; the miracle of a publican become an evangelist; the miracle, finally, of legions of martyrs who remained firm in their innocence and in the confession of their Faith when the world not only tormented them but subjected them to torture in a thousand ways.

To practice true Christianity is to serve God with purity of intention to the limit of our capacity, and thus to walk in the way of holiness. Hence, moving from "virtue to virtue," we shall pass "from the valley of tears" to the place of eternal delight. Then death will no longer be a hideous monster from which we flee in terror, but the good angel come to close our tired eyes after a hard day of labor, to bring us into the abode of rest, to reveal to us the eternal vision "which makes man happy."

Grace: the Countersign to Heaven

Grace is synonymous with charity; hence charity becomes a password to heaven. Christianity is founded upon charity: the charity of God, the charity of our Savior, Jesus, the reciprocal charity of Christians. It is the charity of God the Father! For what is all of creation if not an act of infinite charity? It is God's goodness which extends itself into the void and fills it with innumerable creatures. It is the charity of God the Son! What else is the redemption if not mercy which forgives, rehabilitates, uplifts and saves? And what else is the sanctification of the soul if not the loving work of God the Holy Spirit, through whom the flower of holiness, unfolded by the warmth of life-giving grace, develops into the fruit of eternal life in the heart of man?

The work of creation, of the redemption, of the sanctification of souls would be inexplicable if we did not keep in mind the nature of God, who is charity by èssence: "God is love..." (1 John 4:16). All creation is born of love, teaches love, and leads to love.

Created to the image and likeness of God, the Christian must live by charity — that charity which gives and fulfills itself for the good of one's brethren. Upon the heart of the Christian must be engraved the image of the Father holding the bleeding body of His Son, who, in turn, extends His pierced hands toward mankind in an embrace of infinite charity. Charity is the sign of all Christians. Jesus has said: "This is how all will know you for my disciples: your love for one another" (Jn. 13:35).

A certain author once observed: "It (charity) is a natural characteristic in those who are members of the Mystical Body of Him who loved us to the point of giving Himself. If a piece of metal is attracted by a strong magnet, it, in turn, attracts another piece, then another, and another, and it forms a chain; but, if it does not attract, it is a sign that of itself it lacks attraction."

The charity of Jesus Christ cannot help but make us like unto Him, who is infinite charity. And if we do not have charity, it is a sign that we ourselves are not attracted and, hence, are cut off from Him. As the entire life of the Church abounds in mercy, pardon and love, so must the life of its members abound. What kind of Christian is he who does not love, does not pity, does not forgive?

Now, the flower of charity which is sprouted here below, in the fertile bosom of the Church, blossoms in heaven, in the embrace of God.

What is heaven if not the kingdom of charity? Only in that kingdom will the two extremities of the spiritual world — the immensity of God and our littleness —

enfold one another in a miracle of charity, and the inhabitants of heaven will celebrate this miracle in an eternal triumph of love. The last judgment will be made on the basis of charity, and the "blessed of the Father" will bear the seal of mercy and pardon. The infinite charity of God will welcome His children into the paternal mansion, and the children's charity will give them the right to enter.

An Absolutely Necessary Means

It is a common doctrine of the theologians—St. Basil, St. John Chrysostom, St. Augustine and others—that prayer by adults is not only a precept but also a necessary means for entering the kingdom of heaven; that is, a believer cannot ordinarily save himself if he does not have recourse to God to ask of Him the grace necessary for salvation. St. Thomas affirms: "After Baptism, continuous prayer is necessary to man in order for him to go to heaven."

In his work, *The Great Means of Prayer,* St. Alphonsus de Liguori said that all those who save themselves, speaking of adults, ordinarily save themselves by prayer; and then he proceeds to give the reason. In fact, without the aid of grace, we cannot do anything good: "...apart from me you can do nothing" (Jn. 15:5). Moreover, St. Paul said that we cannot even *begin* to desire it: "It is God who, in his good will toward you, begets in you any measure of desire or achievement" (Phil. 2:13).

Now then, if, on the one hand, we cannot do anything without the aid of grace, and if God ordinarily grants this aid only to those who pray, it is evident that prayer is an absolutely necessary means for saving oneself.

"God is love…" (1 Jn. 4:16).
All creation is born of love,
teaches love, and leads to love.

St. Alphonsus wrote a little book to prove this truth, a booklet which he considered highly useful for everyone, and he declared it to be superior to all spiritual treatises. It is this booklet that the holy doctor wished to see in the hands of all the faithful: "If I could, I would want to print as many copies of this little book as there are faithful living on earth, and give it to each, so that all of us might understand the necessity of praying in order to save ourselves."

A Morally Necessary Means

It was the holy St. Alphonsus, more than anyone else, who pointed out to Christians this absolutely essential means for attaining eternal salvation; and it was also he who called attention to another moral necessity: devotion to the Blessed Mother. "Devotion to the Blessed Virgin," said St. Alphonsus, "is morally necessary for salvation, and this for the same reason given to prove the necessity of prayer."

To be saved, we must have grace. Now, we know that, according to the plan of the redemption, grace comes to us through Mary, Mediatrix of all graces; hence, the necessity of having recourse to our heavenly Mother.

St. Alphonsus proved the point of this doctrine in his book, *The Glories of Mary*. "The point we aim to prove," he said, "is that the intercession of Mary is also necessary for our salvation; necessary we say, not absolutely, but morally, to speak properly. And we say that this necessity is born of the very will of God, who desires that all the graces which He dispenses should pass through the hands of Mary."

Oh, the devotion to the Blessed Mother! What a guarantee for heaven!

Sometimes a mere homage faithfully practiced is enough to secure the protection of our most tender Mother. The story is told that a devout woman, dressed in mourning, presented herself to the saintly Curé of Ars to commend to him the soul of her husband, who had died without receiving the sacraments.

"He was indifferent. He did not practice his religion," the woman sobbed. "What will have become of him?"

"Madame," replied the Curé kindly, "don't you remember the bouquet of flowers which he used to bring from the country every Saturday to beautify the altar of Mary? Know, then, that our Lady has rewarded him by having him make an act of perfect contrition at the point of death, by which the blessed soul of your husband was enabled to soar to heaven."

No less great is Mary's protection of those who faithfully recite three "Hail Mary's" in her honor daily. This little practice, earnestly recommended to everyone, is a golden thread which will help us not to lose our way in the desert of this world. At least, if we do become lost, we shall be able to find again the road that leads to the Father's mansion.

To know the Virgin Mother, to imitate her virtues, to call upon her in that prayer so dear to her, the holy Rosary, is equivalent to securing for ourselves a place in heaven. The Church attributes to her what the Word of God, the Wisdom of the Father, says of Himself: "So now, O children, listen to me; instruction and wisdom do not reject! Happy the man who obeys me, and happy those who keep my ways, happy the man watching daily at my gates, waiting at my doorposts; For he who finds me finds life, and wins favor from the Lord..." (Prv. 8:32-35).

St. Germain addressed the Virgin with these affectionate and true words: "No one is delivered from evil if not through you, most immaculate Lady! No one receives a blessing if not through you, most merciful Lady! No one attains final victory if not through you, most holy Lady."

How consoling is this last appeal! How tremendous is the moment of death, because upon it depends our eternal destiny.

In that terrible moment the dying person, forgetful of the world which is disappearing before his eyes, calls for his mother.

We have seen people over eighty die with the name "mother" on their lips.

Beside a young sailor, found dead together with twenty-six other victims in a submarine that had sunk in the waters of Pola, was found a sheet of paper on which was written: "Mother...." Overtaken by death, his hand had stopped writing.

The tragedy of it was that the mother of the poor sailor was far away and unaware, but even had she known, what could she have done?

Such is not the case with our heavenly Mother, however. She can come to our aid in that final hour, and before the dying gaze which seeks her, she presents herself as "a favorable star" and the "gate of heaven." It is because of this that the Church teaches us that consoling plea of the Hail Mary: "Pray for us sinners, now and at the hour of our death!"

Let Us Draw from the Treasure Chest

A soul in the state of grace is a treasure in itself, inasmuch as it is in a position to draw from the great treasures of the Church the "precious pearls of indulgences," as St. Ignatius Loyola called them.

The treasury of the Church consists of the infinite merits of Jesus Christ, of the Blessed Virgin, and of the saints; all the faithful in the state of grace can share in these as they desire by virtue of the most consoling dogma of the communion of saints. Indulgences, as understood by the doctrine of the Church, remit temporal punishment due to sins already confessed and forgiven; they are granted by the legitimate authority out of the treasury of the Church — to the living and the dead.

The conditions for the faithful to gain these indulgences are:

1) to be in the state of grace;

2) to have the intention of gaining a particular indulgence;

3) to do the good works required.

Ordinarily, these comprise confession, holy Communion, prayer according to the intention of our Holy Father, the Pope, and a visit to a certain church or the recitation of a certain prayer.

Many partial and plenary indulgences have been granted by Popes to congregations, to prayers, and to objects of devotion. For example, a plenary indulgence is attached to the recitation of five mysteries of the Rosary in church before the Blessed Sacrament. A plenary indulgence is also granted to the devout practice of the Way of the Cross.

If we were to list all the prayers, good works and devout exercises endowed with indulgences, plenary and partial, we would fill a number of pages. We might simply mention here a few of the brief prayers to which a partial indulgence is attached, if these are recited with humble confidence in God by persons who lift their minds to Him in the performance of their duties and in bearing the trials of life: All for

You — May God be blessed — Your will be done — My God and my all — O God, have mercy on me, a sinner — My Jesus, mercy — Jesus, Mary, Joseph — My Mother, my Hope.

We are also reminded of the privilege attached to membership in the Confraternity of the Scapular of Mt. Carmel, as revealed to Saint Simon Stock on July 16, 1251, at Cambridge, England. The Blessed Virgin handed him the scapular with these consoling words: "Receive, my dear son, the scapular of your Order as the livery of my confraternity. It is a sign of the privilege which I have obtained for you and for all the children of Carmel. He who dies wearing this habit will be preserved from eternal fire; it is a sign of salvation, a defense in peril, a token of peace and of eternal alliance."

Of course, the scapular must be worn with honor and merit in performing good works; this in order to avoid presumption and to deserve the protection of the Blessed Virgin.

God's coming down on earth, His working for thirty years in the humble shop of Nazareth, His undergoing untold humiliation and torment, and finally his dying upon the cross amid the derision and contempt of the rabble — all this seemed not enough for the infinite love of God. He decided to invent countless other means to make our road to His kingdom in heaven easier and swifter.

As the mystical renewal of Calvary — the supreme act of mediation by Christ, our Savior, before the Father — the Holy Mass is mankind's greatest treasure. It is a bottomless reservoir of God's merciful love. Because of it, as from a spring, flow those seven streams of revivifying refreshment, our heritage of the sacraments.

Finally, it would be most prudent for us to secure for ourselves a plenary indulgence for the moment of death.

A zealous soul goes on accumulating treasures of love within itself daily; he who burns with the ardor of love in this life will not burn in the fire of atonement in the next. At parting, this soul will not need to enter the flames of purgatory, but will immediately be admitted to the eternal love of God in heaven.

A Popular Road to Heaven

A secret for winning heaven is the devotion of the nine first Fridays of the month, now almost universally known and practiced. The Sacred Heart of Jesus made this promise to His confidante, St. Margaret Mary Alacoque.

While the devout sister was absorbed in peaceful prayer, a heavenly light shone down upon the altar, and she saw our adorable Savior in the act of showing her His Heart. "Margaret," Jesus said to her, "in the abounding mercy of my Heart I promise you that my love will grant the grace of final perseverance to all who receive Communion on the first Friday of the month for nine consecutive months; they will not die in my displeasure nor without receiving the sacraments, my divine Heart becoming their safe refuge in those last moments."

Hence, we may reasonably believe that a person who has received Holy Communion in a suitable manner on the first Friday of each month for nine consecutive months can have moral certitude of eternal salvation.

The conditions for attaining this "Great Promise," are:

1. *To receive nine Holy Communions.*

(We must be rightly disposed, of course. Above all, we must be in the state of grace.)

2. *To receive on the first Friday of the month.*

(This reception cannot be transferred to any other day of the week. Not even the confessor can change the day or permit an interruption, because the Church has not granted this faculty to anyone.)

3. *To receive for nine consecutive months.*

(If anyone should skip even a single month, he would not be in order. Even though it were not his fault, he would have to start over again.)

Another condition is the intention of making reparation to the Sacred Heart of Jesus for all the offences He suffers in the Blessed Sacrament of His love, and of gaining the fulfillment of the Great Promise. It is enough to declare the intention at the commencement of the nine Communions and an excellent thing to renew the intention each time one receives.

This practice may begin in any month of the year, and other intentions besides the above mentioned may be included. It is permitted also to apply to the souls in purgatory such indulgences as the one granted to those who, before and after receiving Communion on the first Friday of the month, meditate a while upon the infinite goodness of the Sacred Heart of Jesus and pray for the intentions of the Holy Father.

After the first completion of this practice, it would be well to repeat it throughout life. It is enough to declare the intention once and for all and to repeat the devotion as soon as it has been completed.

This repetition is particularly recommended should one doubt whether he has carried out the devotion with the right disposition.

The Golden Key to Heaven

Another efficacious way to secure heaven is by an act of perfect contrition. Some time ago there was published a translation of Father De Driech's pamphlet entitled *The Golden Key to Heaven*, in which he discussed perfect contrition. The author lamented people's lack of knowledge about the devout practice of perfect contrition. He went on to demonstrate its importance and, at times, its necessity.

Perfect contrition is an intense sorrow of the soul, a detestation of all sins committed, inasmuch as they are offenses against God, Supreme Good, infinitely worthy of all our love. The formula which contains this act should run more or less like this: "Lord, I am sorry for having offended You, because You are infinitely good and worthy of all my love, and because sin displeases and offends You." This perfect act of contrition cancels every sin even before one goes to confession, although if one has committed mortal sin, the obligation of going to confession as soon as possible remains. (In the meantime, one is not to receive Communion.)

Repentance prompted by perfect love of God is not hard to feel if one stops to consider God's attributes and His great love for us. How precious is this practice, which in a single instant can reopen the gates of heaven to the greatest sinner! The good thief, who on the cross turned to the dying Redeemer and said to Him, "Lord, remember me when You come into Your kingdom" made a perfect act of contrition, and for this, Jesus answered him: "This day you will be with me in paradise."

One day a poor sinner, touched by the grace of God, went to a holy priest to confess his sins. The confessor welcomed the prodigal son with great kindness, and the penitent told the sad story of his life. The sins confessed were grave in kind and many in number, but the sinner's sorrow was so obvious that the confessor, following the rules of his sacred ministry, saw fit to impose upon him the recitation of only five Our Father's as a penance.

Amazed, the man exclaimed, "Father, are you giving me so small a penance for such enormous sins?"

At this, the confessor, now even more convinced of the deep sorrow of his penitent, said, "Well, now, it will be enough for you to recite only *one* Our Father, since, I assure you, because of the perfect contrition you have for your sins, the Lord does not ask more."

Having heard this, the penitent dropped dead out of pure sorrow for his sins. Truly, here was a perfect act of contrition and, for that fortunate sinner, the "golden key to heaven!"

The practice of perfect contrition is precious, especially nowadays, on account of the frequency of sudden deaths and industrial accidents. The author of the previously-mentioned pamphlet relates of himself: "One day I was in danger of imminent death; I had only eight or ten seconds left before the end would come for me. In this brief moment a thousand thoughts passed through my mind. With lightning swiftness, my entire life presented itself to me, together with the thought of what awaited me after death — all that, I repeat, in the brief duration of eight or ten seconds. Fortunately my life was saved.

"What was my first concern when faced with that imminent danger of death?

"It was to make an act of contrition with fervent recourse to God's protection.

"It was precisely in that moment that I learned to love and highly esteem perfect contrition...." And he added, "What an irreparable loss the failure of knowing the value of it can bring about in that critical moment! During an accident, nothing is heard but wailing and weeping. People lose their heads; the doctor or the priest is called; all kinds of remedies at hand are hastily applied; but, in the meantime, the victim of the accident is in agony, and perhaps no one thinks of the victim's immortal soul. No one suggests making an act of perfect contrition."

Without doubt, the knowledge and practice of the act of perfect contrition have opened the gates of heaven to a multitude of souls otherwise exposed to eternal damnation. Meanwhile, constantly practiced by faithful souls, perfect contrition admirably increases the life of grace within them.

Fortunate, then, is he who knows how to take advantage of this golden key during his lifetime. Fortunate is he, who, before closing his eyes at night and abandoning himself to sleep, recalls the events of the day and asks God's pardon with an act of perfect contrition. He will open for himself the gates of heaven. If death should overtake him during the night, his soul will find itself ushered into the kingdom of the blessed. For him death will indeed be, as a Spanish writer once described the death of the just: "a falling asleep among men to reawaken among the angels."

Life Is a Vocation for Heaven

We are called to heaven! It is ours by inheritance. We are children of God, and God has promised heaven to us as a reward for the good works we do—"the crown of justice."

Heaven is ours: we have the vocation for it! Jesus found Peter and Andrew on the shore of Lake Genesareth and He called them saying, "I will make you fishers of men." Leaving all, they followed Him. Later on, He called James and John: "Come follow me," and, leaving relatives and possessions, they too followed Him. He then called Nathaniel, Philip, and the other disciples.

One day, Peter asked Him what someone who had left everything to follow Him would receive in compensation, and Jesus answered: He "...will receive many times as much and inherit everlasting life" (Mt. 19:29).

On the road to Damascus, the same Jesus stopped Saul, struck him down from his horse and, in an instant, changed his thoughts, heart and his will. He called Saul to suffer with Him and to spread His name everywhere. What was the recompense to be? St. Paul tells us: "I have fought the good fight, I have finished the race, I have kept the faith. From now on a merited crown awaits me; on that Day the Lord, just judge that he is, will award it to me..." heaven! (2 Tm. 4:7-8)

St. Thomas, the great and principal theologian and philosopher of the Church, was once asked by the Lord what he wanted in recompense for his precious and numerous writings. Thomas replied, "I want nothing else, Lord, but You, Your heaven."

Millions of martyrs follow the King of martyrs, Jesus Christ, even to bloody immolation. Heroes, why do you follow Jesus? What will the Divine Master give you?

Jesus answers: "Life everlasting," heaven!

Of Agnes, Agatha, Lucy, God asked their youth, their virginity, life itself. Of Him who asked such precious gifts, the virgins asked, "What will You give us in exchange?" And He: "I will give you heaven."

Jesus' invitation is always the same: "Come follow me...you will receive a hundredfold and life everlasting."

If the sons and daughters of Cottolengo had asked, "Why do you have us leave everything and make us live a most mortified life, always among the sick?" the answer would have been, "For heaven."

If the followers of any religious founder were to ask, "Why have you made us leave everything and called us to a life of hardship and penance?" the answer would be: "To give you a beautiful heaven."

What will the Lord give us at the end of a life full of hardship and toil, misery and privation, pain and anguish? He will give us heaven. "Rejoice and exult," said the Lord, "for great is your reward in heaven."

Heaven is the reward meted out in proportion to the labor of each. Heaven awaits every labor, every tear, every good deed.

When at the point of death, St. Francis of Assisi had himself laid on the ground. "Why am I still on earth?" he asked. "The just are awaiting me."

When, according to St. Paul, our earthly habitation is dissolved, when, like him, we shall have fought the good fight and reached the end of our race with the torch of our faith brightly aglow, we, too, shall receive from the just Judge the crown of justice in that eternal mansion, "not made by human hands," in heaven.

> *Sursum corda:* let us lift up our hearts as we go
> through the flowery paths
> of hope
> to the eternal fields, —
> to the reward
> which surpasses our hopes!

Napoleon said to his soldiers who were about to go into battle in Egypt, "Remember that from the top of these pyramids forty centuries are looking down upon you."

O Christian, from heaven above, God, the Blessed Virgin, and the saints are looking down on you. A heaven of delight shines over your head. The saints extend their arms toward you and show you the trophies of victory; and Christ, the risen Savior, He who redeemed you, points to the place that He has prepared for you.

A short time and then...heaven will be yours!

While you wait, nothing remains for you but to extend your arms toward our brothers who are already inhabitants of heaven, and to pray to them as St. Augustine once did:

"O all you happy saints of Zion, who already have journeyed through the deep vale of this mortality and have merited to reach the haven of perpetual rest, of perpetual safety, of perpetual peace — you who are forever secure and tranquil, forever happy — I pray you in your charity, because you are secure for yourselves, to be also concerned about us.

"You who are secure in your incorruptible glory, be also concerned about us in our manifold misery.

"Pray for us, your brothers, so that, helped by your prayers, we, too, may arrive with a ship full of cargo in the harbor of perpetual salvation, security!"

Daughters of St. Paul

IN MASSACHUSETTS
  50 St. Paul's Avenue, Boston, Ma. 02130
  172 Tremont Street, Boston, Ma. 02111
IN NEW YORK
  78 Fort Place, Staten Island, N.Y. 10301
  625 East 187th Street, Bronx, N.Y. 10458
  525 Main Street, Buffalo, N.Y. 14203
IN NEW JERSEY
  84 Washington Street, Bloomfield, N.J. 07003
IN CONNECTICUT
  202 Fairfield Avenue, Bridgeport, Ct. 06603
IN OHIO
  2105 Ontario St. (at Prospect Ave.), Cleveland, Oh. 44115
  25 E. Eighth Street, Cincinnati, Oh. 45202
IN PENNSYLVANIA
    1719 Chestnut St., Philadelphia, Pa. 19103
IN FLORIDA
  2700 Biscayne Blvd., Miami, Fl. 33137
IN LOUISIANA
  4403 Veterans Memorial Blvd.,
    Metairie, La. 70002
  86 Bolton Avenue, Alexandria, La. 71301
IN MISSOURI
  1001 Pine St. (at North 10th), St. Louis, Mo. 63101
IN TEXAS
  114 East Main Plaza, San Antonio, Tx. 78205
IN CALIFORNIA
  1570 Fifth Avenue, San Diego, Ca. 92101
  278 17th Street, Oakland, Ca. 94612
  46 Geary Street, San Francisco, Ca. 94108
IN HAWAII
  1184 Bishop St., Honolulu, Hi. 96813
IN ALASKA
  750 West 5th Avenue
  Anchorage, Ak. 99501
IN CANADA
  3022 Dufferin Street, Toronto 395, Ontario, Canada
IN ENGLAND
  57, Kensington Church Street, London W. 8, England
IN AUSTRALIA
  58, Abbotsford Rd., Homebush, N.S.W., Sydney 2140,
    Australia